THEOLOGY *of* HOME IV

THEOLOGY *of* HOME IV

ARRANGING *the* SEASONS

EMILY MALLOY

Foreword by

CARRIE GRESS & NOELLE MERING

TAN Books
Gastonia, North Carolina

Photography by Emily Malloy
Cover design by David Ferris—www.davidferrisdesign.com

ISBN: 978-1-5051-2794-2
Kindle ISBN: 978-1-5051-2795-9
ePUB ISBN: 978-1-5051-2796-6

Published in the United States by
TAN Books
PO Box 269
Gastonia, NC 28053
www.TANBooks.com

Printed in India

For Timothy Crewe—
your tireless, sacrificial, and loving devotion
made this journey possible.

Thank you for all of your yeses.

"Never lose an opportunity
of seeing anything beautiful,
for beauty is God's handwriting."

–RALPH WALDO EMERSON.

Contents

Preface

Dietrich von Hildebrand mused years ago about craftsmen attending to the smallest details when building cathedrals. As one story goes, a rich man noted a worker giving hours upon hours to carving a tiny bird onto a wood beam that would eventually be covered by the roof. The wealthy man's expressed bewilderment was met by a simple response from the worker. "God sees it," he reminded him with simplicity.

This story illuminates the importance of our hidden lives, when love is poured into details that seemingly go unnoticed. We rightfully marvel at the heroic bravery of martyrs, but we also canonize great souls like Saint Therese of Lisieux whose life was small both in duration and geographical scope, but expansive interiorly with ripples and fruits that we will not know in this life and that are surely unraveling still. Even her moniker, "the Little Flower," ties together this sense of tininess with great expansive love.

Though she is more commonly connected to roses, a less sung flower, lantana, illustrates this tiny and expansive connection quite well. Originally a tropical flower, it is now propagated widely. Its small pops of vibrant colors dot paths and sidewalks in cities and rural towns alike. What appears at first to be a single flower on each stem upon examination turns out to be a host of tiny florets intricately clustered together and unified by one main stem into a little dome shape. It is easy to miss, such that it can take a curious toddler to stop and crouch and pluck before we really see the design and details. Even then, it is often picked apart in those tiny hands too quickly to preserve.

What are we to make of such things other than that, of course, a loving God who sees and rejoices in the unseen acts of love by us will also certainly have beaten us to the punch? It is fitting that He would create a world with such wonders as large as the ocean and as hidden as tiny, luminescent deep-sea creatures, or the minuscule details of a single, ephemeral lantana stem.

Were we to attempt to sculpt or craft these miniscule details to create one single stem of lantana, it would take painstaking work, be priced accordingly, and then preserved under a cloche. We attempt such detailed love as the woodworker with his bird or mother with her child, but we casually trample over the detailed handiwork of a single flower that we have no capacity to replicate ourselves.

Perhaps this is one part of why we associate flowers with love: the love a gardener pours into cultivating them, their marking of weddings and funerals alike, and the birthdays and dinners and every holiday in between and around.

In this volume, Emily Malloy explores the vibrancy and life of the garden, and how its incorporation into our homes is more significant than the practical efforts of cutting, arranging, and displaying. Though such work is addressed in these pages as well, it is the deeper questions of life, family, love, and God that animates her work and all of ours as we strive in simple and small ways to layer our lives and homes with the intangibles that turn the stuff of matter into a song.

While there are plenty of good treatments on floral design and garden life, so often the meaning behind their creation is overlooked. We can't think of anyone better to pull together this amazing work. To it, she brings her background in floral arranging, food blogging, photography, her elegant eye, and her devotion to the Faith.

At first glance, a serious treatment of flowers might seem surprising. But like the lantana or the bird carving, real richness can be found in the

seemingly insignificant. Perhaps giving our attention to their details can help make us more attentive to our own—the small stirrings within us and others that connect one to another and to Him, and the details of love that we do well to dignify.

A new way to go deeper into a Theology of Home.

Carrie Gress
Noelle Mering

Paperwhites to Pines

The gentle caress of a chilly breeze pushes wisps of hair into my face as I snip paperwhites, marking the celebration of New Year's Eve. Each stem clutches several sweet little fragrant blooms. I take in this delicate beauty with all its lovely details and recall that this little stem was created for joy.

A decade ago, when I began working with flowers, I did not understand how they could demonstrate true beauty and accentuate the world's deep longing for it. Nor could I have foreseen how they provide a deepened understanding of the love of God. But in these ten years, He has mercifully shown me the beautiful parallels between flowers and life and the endless lessons nature provides.

Meditating upon the delicate splendor of the lilies of the field, I am reminded that the God who created this immense wonder sees humanity as the pinnacle of His creation. As my scissors cut through the stems of paperwhites, gathered for an arrangement, I think of the floral calendar and remember its botanic beauty. Each flower is a gift of love from the Father to accompany us through the days that accumulate into months. With each season comes a new, lovely fragrant friend to remind us that though time is an uncontrollable force, with it comes endless unique gifts that were unavailable yesterday.

Flowers escort us through time; they have journeyed with all humankind, just as they were there in Eden. In this, flowers point to the innate need for beauty sewn into the foundation of our being. We were formed to reside with God amid the splendor of the garden. It is intrinsic to the human heart. We see it even in those with a secular worldview who seek to "recharge" in nature. Wittingly or not, mankind's time in nature is a divine encounter. Flowers represent all that is good and wondrous in nature. And in turn, they serve as a powerful representation of the gifts we receive from God.

Flowers: A Proud Assertion

"Flowers are a proud assertion," said Ralph Waldo Emerson, "that a ray of beauty outvalues all the utilities of this world." What is the use of beauty? Beauty has no particular use in terms of concrete measurability, which is why modernity, steeped in utility, seeks to move beyond it. But it is precisely because it is of "no particular use" that it is so crucial. Utility serves some other end, an end that asserts that things are consumables and that humans are merely consumers. Beauty cannot be consumed but only happened upon or created. The eyes that encounter beauty can only be affected and changed by it. As Peter Kreeft has said, "Beauty is the first thing we notice and love." Saint Thomas Aquinas defined beauty as "that which, upon being seen, pleases." How could we even begin to quantify that which expands our hearts? Such a thing cannot be measured scientifically.

The beauty of a bloom is not easily measured or controlled. A flower just *is*, and because of its simplicity, we delight in it. Yet it also assists in making tangible in the created world that which is unseen but still *is*. "Beauty contains a summons," said Dietrich von Hildebrand, "it awakes awe in us; it elevates us above which is base; it fills our hearts with a longing for the eternal beauty of God." Beauty exists in great cathedrals and works of art, drawing our yearning hearts toward heaven. Yet it also exists in the simple beauty of the flower. God has gifted us a unique opportunity to know Him more deeply through the admiration of the work of His hands. What we cannot see in God we can see in His creation.

Our modern lives are busy. In our harried pace, there is little time to be recollected. Stopping to "smell the roses" makes possible the fulfillment of spiritual needs by meditating upon the transcendent. This slowing permits an encounter with God, rooting us in place, elevating the ordinary.

At Home with Beauty

Among the innate desires of human beings, there are two that supersede the others: the desire for sustenance, and the other for beauty. Without sustenance, we perish. Without beauty, we cease to be human. An ancient Chinese proverb says that "when you only have two pennies left in the world, buy a loaf of bread with one, and a lily with the other." Master gardener Monty Don states that even in lean times, peasants made sure to always plant flowers in their gardens since they were viewed, too, as a necessity. Their universally beguiling beauty transcends time, culture, and economic status.

"Beauty be not caused—it is."

—EMILY DICKINSON

Like the peasants, we intuit that our homes should be places not only of sustenance and shelter but also of beauty. Home is foundational in the formation of hearts. This formation has a rippling effect, spilling over to the outside world. Women often possess a unique ability to bring beauty into the home. We set up the house, adorn the walls, and seek to create a backdrop for endless memories. God has done the same for us in the created world. The world is a garden within which He seeks to mold us. We adorn our homes with the same communication of love; through seemingly unimportant external signs, we elicit an inward feeling out of the ordinary.

When we arrange flowers, we gather what exists in nature to create a new reality. Flower arrangements, like cathedrals, draw our hearts toward the transcendent. Using the created materials in conjunction with each other forms a new whole that draws our minds and hearts to the one who created each piece. A stone alone is an ordinary object, but when arranged in harmony and order with other materials, it creates magnificent cathedrals that aid in the contemplation of the One who created and willed not just the stone but also the artists. So, too, as we contemplate the beauty of a flower, we comprehend through the delicate nature of each petal, stock, stamen, that God is intentional with every intricate detail. Like the building of a great cathedral, the building of a flower arrangement, stem by stem, creates a masterpiece. The layers of foliage are the stonewall backdrop, the supporting flowers are like the buttresses, all working in harmony to showcase the focal blooms which sit like stained-glass windows. Creative works pay powerful homage to the Creator, opening a new door to the transcendent.

"One can dream so much better in a room
where there are pretty things."

–LUCY MAUD MONTGOMERY

Design articles often speak of the importance of bringing the outside in. Less common is an acknowledgment that we were created for the experience of beauty. Without this deep understanding of the importance of beauty in our lives, and consequently, within our homes, these articles remain superficial. When we bring nature inside, however, we create a new Eden within our homes where our Lord can reside. A home can be a sacred place filled with ordinary glimpses of hidden life. As we permit flowers to be a part of daily life, we can contemplatively reside within our homes and pause—even if just for a moment—at the sight of beauty. Their fleeting nature prompts us

to stop, reflect, and gaze, however briefly. In these moments of stillness, the Lord works.

This book is meant to rekindle the deep relationship between women and those most treasured fruits of nature: flowers. It is meant to remind us to bask in the beauty of this great gift. The waters of the world, the fruit-bearing tree, and the blooming rose provide abundant life and nourishment not for themselves but for every living thing.

I stoop down one last time to take in the sweet scent of paperwhite flowers poking through the chilled earth. It is amazing to sense the intensity of fragrance emitted by just one tiny bloom.

A gift for the New Year.

Many say time is a thief, but when viewed through the seasonal lens of ever-changing gifts, it accrues. As the paperwhites fade, we get the buzz and bloom of spring, the swelter of summer, and the marveling death of autumn. When the calendar year ends, we deck the halls of our domestic churches with fragrant pine and red ribbons. All the time that passes between paperwhites and pines reminds us of the transformative power of beauty.

Journey with me through the seasons, marveling in God's gift of flowers.

WINTER

A deep stillness envelopes the earth in winter. Even though winter is different for each climate, much of the refrain remains the same: dormancy, hibernation, silence. In some regions of the world, there are a few brave, though scarce, flowers to welcome the outdoor wanderer. Under the crisp, frost-bitten landscape, pansies, leucojum, snowdrops, camellias, and hellebores perfume the thin, cold air.

It may seem strange to begin a floral book with the season devoid of flowers. An argument can be made that such a book should begin with spring, a time of birth, a season of the loveliest flowers. I would argue, however, that it feels as if we were skipping over the difficult moments and heading straight to the easiest, which hardly serves as a realistic reflection of life. The warmth of a spring sun means so much more after the cold. With each February day, our hearts steadily grow in anticipation of verdant pastures. March's arrival brings the desire to a fever pitch, setting a meditative framework as we see the wonder of growth in places that once laid barren.

The rhythm of the seasons enhances our anticipation of what is not present. In it, we can marvel and find joy in the arrangement of God's created order. Creation isn't a series of accidents or coincidences but structured with divine intentionality. Nature and its beauty are a conglomeration of extraordinary solos within various movements that come together to form a symphony, a love song from a Father to His children.

Living with an intentional view of the seasons cultivates patience in the onlooker, a patience that spills over into various aspects of life by living in the present season and the fruits it brings. We wait, knowing what is to come. A bud opens to a flower only once and at a particular time of the year. Though a season may seem short to us, all that nature does is according to an ordained purpose, and is, therefore, always on time. Unlike a mother who is always harried for time, in the seasons, we witness the miraculous because nature never rushes. It is always on time. The lesson is clear: each life happens only once and is timed for a purpose.

With the daily deliveries of flowers from South America, Africa, and Europe, we forget that specific flowers only bloom at certain times. I am an advocate for seasonal blooms, growing or buying. Often emphasized are the environmental benefits of seeking seasonality in arranging—but I want to dig a little deeper (forgive the pun) to consider the importance of waiting and seeing specific beauty blooming in its own time.

"In the cold solitude of winter, I thank the Lord for this opportunity for reflection."

—WINSLOW HOMER

There is so much more to flowers than meets the eye. They speak to deeper realities often overlooked, such as our innate need for beauty; a flower's ability to make beauty accessible fills that deep-seated need. As we become acutely aware in winter, it is in the absence and reemergence of something that we often come to recognize its value. Beauty without meaning can be superficial, but we enter a deeper, transcendent reality when it has a purpose—namely, willing the best of the other.

The Catholic Church is a home for seasonal living. The liturgical calendar dissects the year into six seasons to help us focus and be present. During certain seasons, the parts of the Mass slightly change, but the visuals—linens and vestment colors and so much more—often point to the time of year. The liturgical calendar marks time, as does nature. People used to regularly speak of saints' feasts as calendar markers, such as Michaelmas, when referring to the times of year. The rhythm of the seasons dictates life—as do the seasons of fasting and feasting. These small shifts in routine—for instance seeing a priest in red vestments—help our focus hone in on the present moment.

"Adopt the pace of nature;
her secret is patience."
–RALPH WALDO EMERSON

The domestic church also lives a life of cycles that mimic the Mother Church, as it too is a sacred space. Home life also has its rhythm—summertime freedom marked by jumping through sprinklers differs from the cozy enjoyment of fireside cocoa. We also can have a rhythm to the life of our home accentuated by flowers. Seasonality dictates the backdrop. A simple vase of flowers signifies the time of year while enhancing the beauty of the life lived within the home sanctuary. A seasonally lived life does wonders for the ability to savor the present.

Despite the absence of flowers in winter, a different kind of beauty abounds. Though I long for the wonder of the diverse types of fritillaria blooms with their unmatched shapes and form, I have come to appreciate the unique loveliness of this season. Frost and snow on last summer's flowers sit like sculptures dotting the landscape. Birds perching on branches and their humble little nests are more evident, no longer hidden by leaves. Trellises lie bare in anticipation of being overrun by climbing flowers. It is a time of waiting and watching, because we know that soon the flowers will come. The barrenness seeds our hope. As we turn through the pages of winter, we witness the slow reawakening of nature and the beauty it possesses.

When we live life in this manner, we attune our hearts and senses to the splendor that is right outside the door. Each month contains within it a beautiful story of the natural world, ranging from region to region and changing daily, though always remaining the same in its parade through time. This is a beauty far from mundane. How joyful are those first rays of light after a rainy and moody sky? Again, we see this pattern mimicked in our spiritual life when, after an arid winter of the soul, we are given a grace of consolation. A deeper appreciation of the seasons, with its cycles, is born within us in the stillness of the winter.

The Home Florist's Tool Kit

Arranging flowers at home is simple; all we need are a few items that fill the home florist's tool kit and the knowledge of each item's proper use. For many joyful years, I worked at a bustling flower shop in Philadelphia. I began as an apprentice whose main job was to sweep the shop floors and "process" flowers as they arrived. Over time, I worked my way up the ladder to manage the flower shop and design weddings. At the flower shop, each florist would have a tool kit (and would often don a tool belt as we worked) that held the tools needed to create an arrangement. Such a kit (and belt) can be easily replicated at home.

In my early days as a professional florist, I was only permitted to use a knife to remove leaves and thorns, give fresh cuts to the bottoms of stems, and arrange flowers. Fortunately, snips have come such a long way that they have replaced a knife and band-aids, as rose stems weren't the only recipients of fresh cuts! The sharpness of any item—whether a paring knife, snips, or pruner—is critical. It prevents the stems from being crushed while being cut.

Such tools become an extension of the florist. They do the work our hands are incapable of. There are only a handful of items needed, and they can easily be found in most homes:

- *Pruners* or *clippers* are a great tool to use to cut thick stems or branches. They are a well-rounded, all-purpose item and can be used across the full floral spectrum. Having a sharp cutting tool on hand to cut stems is better than typical paper scissors since trying to cut thicker stems can break the scissors and crush the stems. Always make sure to clean your pruners or clippers after use to ensure that no bacteria grows and spreads.

- *Flower snips* are wonderful to have on hand for trimming more delicate stemmed flowers because they tend to be a great deal sharper than typical pruners. Their scissor shape makes for a comfortable and familiar process of trimming stems. Like pruners or clippers, it's good to consistently keep your flower snips clean. And a paring knife if you are a daring purist!

- There are several forms of *floral tape* available to purchase, and each has a different use. Waterproof tape is a must-have item when arranging in wide-mouthed containers, whether you are forming a grid to hold flowers or to secure balled-up chicken wire. There is also a floral tape with a unique adhesive that is used when constructing bouquets, boutonnieres, and flower crowns. While not a necessity, it can be great to have available should you decide to make a flower crown for a May crowning. It should be noted that this type of tape is not waterproof and, therefore, not helpful in the use of securing flowers in wide-mouthed container arrangements.

- *Wires* are great to have available for several uses. Coated wire and/or a 26-gauge wire are useful in the construction of boutonnieres, garlands, swags, and flower crowns. They have even been wonderfully helpful in reinforcing or repairing injured flower stems.

- *Chicken wire* has become one of the most prominent ways of supporting flowers in wide-mouthed containers. Bowls, urns, and other large opening vases can be difficult to arrange without some sort of mechanism to hold the flowers in place. Chicken wire is also extremely helpful in creating hanging wall installations, as it is lightweight and easy

to work with. All you need is a small spool of chicken wire. Coated wire is best because it doesn't rust, but traditional metal chicken wire works just as well.

- *Frogs* are equally helpful in holding the stems in wide-mouthed containers, like chicken wire. They are adhered to the bottom center of the vessel with a putty. The prongs of the frog pierce and hold the bottom of the flowers in place.

- *Wire cutters* are a necessity when trimming chicken wire down to size. I have used (and damaged!) perfectly good pruners by cutting chicken wire down, but it was extremely difficult.

- Tucking in a pack of *rubber bands* is great in the florist's tool-box to help secure bouquets and gather bunches of stems to hang to dry.

Other items that are more outside the box but still helpful to have as you dive deeper into floral design include:

- *Sheet moss* is always added to my recommendations of helpful items to have on hand. It is not a typical inclusion for a florist tool kit, but it really should be a staple in every home. Moss is useful in so many ways: I've used it to hide chicken wire in less dense flower arrangements, as a floral foam alternative, to wrap the exterior of vases to give an arrangement a "woodland" appearance, tucked it into grapevine wreaths, and so much more. Very few things give a more natural, grown appearance to a design than beautiful green sheet moss.

- A *Lazy Susan* is another great bonus item to have on hand for floral design. Placing your vase on top of the turntable makes it easier to obtain a constant 360-degree view of your design.

While I have used floral foam a great deal in my years of arranging, I have moved away from using it unless necessary (summer outdoor wedding receptions with floral hanging installations wouldn't survive long without it). Chicken wire shaped into a ball and placed into a vase has become a more popular option, and for a good reason. Chicken wire has staying power and is a more sustainable and economical way of arranging flowers since wet floral foam has a once-and-done usage, and is considered toxic. Moreover, arranging flowers in wide-mouthed urns, bowls, and containers is much easier with the chicken wire and frog structure and secured with a bit of floral tape. Not all vases require a structural element to hold flowers, only wide-mouthed containers like bowls and urns.

These items needed for a home florist kit can be sourced online, at garden centers, or in most flower shops. Very little is required for success in floral design; it is one of the most accessible creative outlets to undertake as it demands very little investment. The reward floral design provides, however, is excellent!

January

Christina Rosetti's well-known poem "In the Bleak Mid-winter," put to music by Gustav Holst, is an ode to those austere and beautiful moments of winter that feel reminiscent of January: "frosty wind made moan / earth stood hard as iron / water like the stone; / Snow had fallen, snow on snow / snow on snow." The world holds its breath across the lands of the earth as it falls into rest until it exhales at the first buds of spring.

Nature seems to sleep under frosted blades of grass and hardened ground. The farmer's fallow fields lie in waiting. In the dark and dreary days of winter, all looks desolate as the world is in frozen repose. Do not mistake the quiet for inaction during these winter months. We must not overlook the necessity of the cold, as it helps produce the beautiful bulbs of spring. As H. Rider Haggard stated in *A Farmer's Year*, "Frost in moderation is a good thing for the land, as it pulverizes the earth and destroys noxious insects by the thousands." The gardener rips the spent annuals to prevent pests and diseases that can manifest on dead plants. Perennials maintain their autumnal haircuts that also prevent disease and stimulate healthy growth in the future. There is a great deal of hidden activity behind the curtain, like between the acts of a play. The stage is being prepared for what is to come.

As nature is hard at work, though veiled, a new hidden work takes place within the home as the eager gardener pours over seed catalogs and prepares for the warmer days to come. The image of bright flowers and sun-drenched gardens makes the imagination run wild! In this time of year, when the days are short and the nights are long, the colors of summer seem a lifetime away. Bare branches hint to what was once there. One could view them as a representation of loss, but it is in the stripped-down landscape that the eye can penetrate farther, into the view where once the leaves obstructed. The exposed grounds enable the gardener to dream and plan in a different manner as a blank slate reveals endless possibilities.

Though there is an absence of botanical blooming in the garden, there is one flower that crosses the threshold of the New Year with us. Paperwhites are the flower of the New Year, their delicate fragrance fills the same air carrying newfound resolutions. They grow indoors in pots in colder regions or bear the chilled winter air as they valiantly bloom outdoors in warmer climates.

"All human wisdom is summed up in two words—
wait and hope."

—ALEXANDRE DUMAS

In winter, snow lays heavy upon the wispy branches of evergreen trees, drifts covering all that was once colorful in the flower beds of Christy Isinger. She is a mother, avid gardener, and floral enthusiast who, come winter, misses her garden, "and the wonder of seeing things grow everyday . . . a true blessing." The frosted landscape of Alberta, Canada, is best enjoyed by gazing through windowpanes as the snow becomes too deep even for a Robert Frost inspired woodland traipse. Her gardens that billow with flowers in June lie in frozen anticipation in January. Her children's short bursts of frigid outings are accented by thawing with cocoa in hand. But within the four walls

of the Isinger home, memories are formed as a succession of forced paper-white flower bulbs and amaryllis adorn windowsills and tables. "The white of paperwhites is perfect for the longing of fresh starts in January," she says. Orange slices are dried and hung from the ice-kissed windows to "bring a spice back to life that has long since faded from the colorful days of summer." The warmth of firelight and the glow of candles break through the darkness of the January sky.

While keeping warm inside, simple glances out the window reveal the skeletons of formerly bushy, green plants. After winter precipitation, the land-scape becomes ice-kissed or snow-toppled and creates an almost sugary and

crystallized appearance. If one braves outdoor exploration to take in the wintry panorama, the frosted wind chills faces and the crunch of snow and ice underfoot give away every step. The vista takes on a heavenly feel as the shapes of snow angels frame the view. The subtle growth of snowdrops gently blends into the landscape.

Winter is one continuous and beautiful *memento mori* (Latin for "remember death") as the bones of a garden that shape its character are laid bare. It serves as a reminder of mortality—a reminder that roots in the present. Just as a flower cannot grow without sturdy and healthy roots, souls require a similar foundation.

These character-shaping bones of the garden take on a serene air under a blanket of freshly fallen snow; a beauty that is fleeting, but nevertheless welcomed. There is a unifying element to snow, as it shrouds all indiscriminately: house, tree, dried flower, and road. A stillness is ever-present as each snowflake descends from the skies to blanket, yet illuminate, the hibernating landscape. All is silent and simple. Still, during this time, much is taking place.

The greatest works take place as fields are fallow and nature conserves its energy. Seeds that have fallen and spread through the winds of autumn work to take root. Those plants whose roots wait underfoot establish and strengthen in these cold months. Winter often has the appearance of desolation. In nature, as well as in the soul of man, it is in those desolate moments that the Lord's preparation and work commence. The abundant beauty is there—it merely hides or comes in unexpected ways. Winter's charm is ever-present as snow collects upon dried hydrangea heads or accentuates blooming hellebores.

After the rush of Christmas has passed and the halls cease to bear festive cheer, we feel a decorative deficiency. Sometimes it is met with relief, sometimes sadness. Either way, in winter, we live in anticipatory hope, rest, and seek comfort in the wait. As the first month of the calendar year ends, we begin to appreciate the simple beauty found in snow drifts and the hue of the evergreens that contrast against the barren landscape.

Design

Winter is a time of texture. The landscape is an endless source of inspiration as grasses, structured foliage, and muted tones rule the day. Artists have dedicated a great deal of time to illustrate the beauty of these untamed months. Yet, it is a soft sleepy melody that flora sings in this season. It is the gathering of textures in varying shades and dried elements that bring the same feeling of realism captured in a romantic painted landscape. A traipse outdoors can produce a wonder of things with which to create. Dried flowers have also become a popular item and are easily sourced. There is still a bounty of wonder to be had; it is just knowing what to seek.

Autumn-planted flora, such as kale, weather the winter and serve as a beautiful focal cut flower. In these restful months, the gardener plots, plans, and prepares, but mostly waits. Beauty cannot be rushed. An outdoor hike

can provide fallen evergreen branches with pinecones still attached. Arrangements throughout the winter can take on more architectural elements by way of dried stems and branches. Despite the lack of blossoming beauty outside at our disposal, there is still a great deal that can be brought in: dried hydrangea stems or poppy pods, interesting branches, and any stem of flower you see blooming, depending upon the region: pansies, paperwhites, leucojum, snowdrops, camellias, and hellebores.

Containers

I could happily write an entire book—or sonnet—about containers. They are of the utmost importance in floral design as these vessels create a home within our homes for flowers. Attractive containers are a wonderful conversation starter.

Types of containers and vases are as varied as flowers, from the common to the unexpected. Anything can be a vessel, so long as it holds water, from a small shot glass to a champagne bucket. Containers are an overlooked process when arranging flowers. I can say that I gave very little thought to them before I became a florist. Now, seeking unique, unexpected containers to use as a home for flowers is a fun pursuit. If it can hold water or retain moisture by a liner or small jar, it can hold flowers!

Thrift stores, antique shops, and Etsy have been great sources for unique containers. One of my favorites is an antique French holy water font I found online. Arranging flowers for Easter within a vessel where so many hands reached for Holy Water is poetic. I also adore putting flowers in little pots made in crafting classes by the little hands that mean so much to me (although I do place a little glass container inside to be sure it won't leak).

As the variety of vases available is as numerous as the flowers they hold, it is easy to see that each serves a different purpose, depending upon where you will place it. Bud vases holding a single bloom or an urn with draping drama and tall spires all evoke the same joy. But they won't always be placed in similar settings. Bud vases are versatile and can be placed anywhere in single or multiple groupings, and while urns can also be versatile, they can be challenging to use as centerpieces for a dining room table. The container will dictate what it can handle and where it should go.

Narrow-mouthed vases require much fewer stems than an open-footed bowl, as they require more flowers to fill the open spaces. The unwritten rule for dinner centerpieces states that they should stand no taller than the length of your elbow to fingertip, to keep from blocking eye contact between guests.

I love displaying my collection of vases. They hold so much possibility and are as dear to me as my China. No matter where your flower containers call home, it is tremendous fun collecting a variety of containers at your disposal when you want to arrange them. Different glass colors, varying shapes, attractive metallic finishes, and even great-shaped food jars or bottles help build a fantastic little collection. Unique, eye-catching containers fuel the creative process and add a one-of-a-kind depth to the arrangement. Often the most enjoyable way to come across new containers is by thrifting, as favorite a pastime as gardening for most women!

FAIR OAKS

Circa
1800

February

The dark days seem to persist as the weeks pass, yet February is a month marked by slow, subtle change. Though it is a forlorn time of year, weak rays of sunlight fight the enduring darkness in earnest. When the snow melts, it reveals shades of melancholy. It is the peak of planning and of looking forward to warmer days. It is the shortest month of the year (which feels like mercy) in which the slightest shifts of sunlight are most obvious. The skies remain gray, and winter sometimes feels inescapable as the pause of the season is felt most in February. Our latent optimism reemerges after the feast of Candlemas when the days grow longer. We know the cold will soon break.

Despite the barrenness of the landscape, in flower shops we find that the abundance of flora never ceases. This brief month ironically serves as the busiest time of year for a florist. Floral celebrations serve as an ode to Saint Valentine and romantic love. Cliché though it may seem, flowers are singular in their expression of love. Saint Valentine's Day traditions bring respite to the winter-weary heart, giving a glimpse of the bounty of life to come.

Although there is beauty in each season, it is a fun distraction to the gray February days to bring home some imported blossoms and be grateful for our contemporary conveniences. It is a floral breakthrough during the leanest time of year. But, for one day—it seems—the world is teaming with flowers, and that is something any flower lover can happily celebrate. Roses

upon roses ship from South America, and interesting bulb flowers make their way across the vast ocean from Holland. Luscious displays of flowers line the shelves in flower shops. Buckets overflow with countless shades of roses containing varying musky notes. Forced bulbs, hothouse flowers, and flowers grown in warmer climates are all available for purchase. Florists are both energized and exhausted by the month of love full of hustle and bustle. This day is akin to Laudate and Gaudete Sundays in which momentary exultation of color and newness breaks into the wait.

Most striking about the secular celebrations of the feast of Saint Valentine is the mirrored imagery in the giving and receiving of beauty through flowers.

There are many stories attributed to Saint Valentine, a third-century priest and martyr, most notably his miraculous healing of a blind girl and the lore of the secret weddings he officiated for Roman soldiers forbidden to wed. The connection of Saint Valentine to romantic love was made during the Middle Ages. These traditions have endured the test of time as the feast day is still marked by gifts of flowers. Love is exchanged between the giver and receiver of blooms. Flowers are foremost an expression of love by God the Father, who made the world a garden for His children. And though we have lost Eden, He still makes available that abundant gift of creation. As February 14 recedes, we are reminded that the days of bustling gardens are long ahead.

"There are always flowers
for those who want to see them."

−HENRI MATISSE

February is also the month that starts our long Lenten fast. The winter season is a fast from flora in much the same way our souls fast from food. When we fast, a deep, unseen growth takes place within our hearts, minds, and souls. It always presents a challenge as we come to terms with our weakness and our needs. Toward the end of this seasonal *memento mori*, we remember our own mortality as ashes are placed upon our foreheads and we are told that we are dust and to dust we shall return. Nothing represents this reality quite like the annual ebb and flow of growth in a landscape.

A common spiritual practice for Lent is to write the word "Alleluia" upon a stone and bury it in the ground, symbolic of its absence in Mass during Lent. In these liturgical observations, we have a heightened awareness of the present; so we have a heightened awareness of the lack of other things in life. When the bells ring and Alleluia's ring out at the Easter Vigil, we are renewed by this new celebration of joy after feeling its long absence.

When I lived in the city, my primary winter barometer was based less upon the look of the landscape and more upon the temperature of the air. Flowers still overflowed in buckets upon the shelves of the flower shop where I worked. I never had to fast from flora alongside the rest of creation. The floral sections of grocery stores still brimmed with blooms grown in distant lands. It was not until I moved to the suburbs—and even more so upon moving deep into the country—that I felt the botanical absence of winter in my bones. I came to realize and appreciate the necessity of this verdant pause.

Though the season is quiet, we expend effort looking beyond the present. Of all four seasons, winter is the most forward-looking time. In

gazing over the horizon wishing for warmer days, we so often miss the opportunity to be moved by the instances of beauty in front of us: foot-prints in the snow, the texture of dried, once-blooming flowers, or the birds' nests exposed in the trees. While the anticipation of warmer days ahead energizes us, the short days remind us to rest in this present time of repose and see that natural beauty and wonder abound in this season. It is only winter that provides a snow-kissed landscape or the wheat color hues of the earth against the moody purple and gray sky; colors that cannot be replicated by the other seasons. Though the harvest is few, the loveliness of the form remains.

"The power of finding beauty
in the humblest of things
makes home happy
and life lovely."

−LOUISA MAY ALCOTT

Despite the dormant state of winter, the most delicate and lovely flow-ers are becoming seasonally available and are well worth the wait. Camel-lias are winter-blooming shrubs that are indispensable to the winter garden. Anemones are singular in their form with striking shades and freckled pet-als. Ranunculi beguile with their endless layers of delicate petals. Loddon lilies and snowdrops quietly and gently hug the cold earth. Hellebores are unusual and gorgeous flowers whose branches make a wonderful addition to any arrangement. These blooms carry us through winter with their soft, layered petals. Oh, how much these first flowers of the calendar year mean to those who have been waiting! These flowers are so subtle and delicate, yet endearing, particularly contrasted to the countless roses and bulb flowers

flown in for Saint Valentine's Day. Yet, as the twenty-eight days of February go by (or twenty-nine during the leap year!), the landscape reveals that, though nature still sleeps, the subtle changes of the month work to prepare the scene for the blooming days to come.

Design

February's designs can take many forms. Of course, Valentine's Day emerges and presents an opportunity for countless flowers that were not previously available. Romantic arrangements overflowing with red roses and other red flowers are apropos. One of my favorite uncommon color palettes is red and peach. The soft warmth of peach enhances red in a beautiful way, similar to what is revealed when biting into a juicy peach.

"If you truly love nature,
you will find beauty everywhere."

—VINCENT VAN GOGH

As fresh flowers emerge from the frozen earth (ranunculus, hellebores, anemones, camellias, snowdrops, and Loddon lily), hopeful arrangements begin adorning the home. I love making use of sage-colored evergreen foliage and dusty miller to shape the arrangement. The bluish green is evocative of the still frozen state of the earth, and the gentle placement of these flowers that seem to arise from the container reflects the same hopeful emergence they have in the garden. It is also enjoyable to take unexpected containers (like an empty maple syrup jar) and place within it a few little celebratory stems of snowdrops or Loddon lily.

Our Secret Gardens

In the well-loved children's classic *The Secret Garden*, we meet Mary Lennox, a sour and unhappy child deprived of love yet indulged with material things according to her whims for her entire life. We witness her heart finally open—like a flower bud—upon her exposure to the beauties and wonders of nature.

The wonder of the seasons and splendor of the flowers, and ultimately life, can have an immense spilling-over effect. Mary's newfound passion for the garden and joy for life become infectious and changes the hardened heart of Colin Craven—her young cousin with similar deprivations and temperament. The story culminates in meeting Colin's father, who neglected him after his wife's death in childbirth. Lord Craven's closing himself off from love upon the tragic death of his wife coincides with his closing of the garden. In shunning beauty, his home becomes one of gloom as he runs to other shores to escape his unhappiness.

This backdrop can apply to our lives as well. Pain can cause us to turn away from even that which might heal us. Authentic beauty pierces our hardened hearts. Mary, Colin, and Lord Craven were affluent and exposed to many forms of beauty, but it wasn't until their encounter with the garden that their hearts changed. As the subtle, natural form of beauty breaks in, so does love. From this love comes a restoration of health and happiness and redemption of relationship, which ripples into their little corner of the world. And so we strive to have life imitate art, growing and tending our own secret gardens where we can disappear into avenues of flowers that, somehow, mysteriously, inspire us to live, and to love.

March

The last month of winter quietly ushers in the first few days of spring. In March, there is a hopeful anticipation rooted in muscle memory. These days are filled with watching. Instinctively we know, even during the coldest of winter nights, that spring always returns. Birds begin to make their reappearance from their winter retreat. Birdsong and subtle smells of dirt increasingly fill the air. It is a month of two seasons. Simultaneously, the buds that begin to form in winter declare the imminence of flowering branches. And yet, as March arrives with its abrupt and prevailing winter winds, its farewell takes a quieted form in the subtle beginnings of vernal splendor.

Few things communicate spring is nearing quite like daffodils. Trumpet-like daffodils announce the softening of the landscape as they break through the ground. They are unique in shape, but very few blooms are similar. Daffodils, like so many bulbs, require the cold for dormancy to produce their beloved beautiful, bright flowers. Their large heads seem to dance in the last of the winter winds, bidding the season adieu. The succession of flowers awakening from their winter slumber continues as crocuses' vibrant color contrasts the dull landscape.

The winds of March—both life-giving and wild—breathe new life into the cold, dry earth. The winds of change can be extremely forceful and intentional in purpose. It is as if we are witnessing a great battle, a collision between two seasons desperate for victory. The book of Genesis comes to

mind: from the great winds over the abyss comes life. Yet, as winter gives way in blustery throes, spring arrives ever so quietly and peacefully. The ice slowly melts to reveal the new growth beneath. Depending upon the location, the end of March reveals the reemergence of green pastures and early spring flowers. Consolation begins as the dark gives way to light, and daylight stretches still further. Trees burst with buds of green giving way to momentous flowers. Forsythia creates a fiery display that almost surprises as it mimics the golden hues of the sun. Tulips quietly rise through the ground, signaling the passing of daffodil season, and slowly evolve from green to colorful displays.

"Daffodils, that come before the swallow dares,
and take the winds of March with beauty."

—WILLIAM SHAKESPEARE

Nothing is sweeter than this month arranged into a vase. How glorious are the blooms' triumphant return after their winter slumber! Their freshness envelopes the home and enraptures the onlooker. Attentiveness grows as each day dawns and brings with it new shades of green and pastel-shaded flowers. The warmth of the sun shining upon the face is reminiscent of those beautiful moments of spiritual consolation after time in the arid desert.

It is in this reawakening that we begin to recognize the value of the beauty and how flowers change us. Simultaneously, we can be present to the wonder emerging all around and maintain a retrospective gaze. The sudden introduction of beauty brings awareness to our once dormant senses.

Flowers can affect all five senses, but also contain the capacity to beguile the mind, stir the heart, and touch the soul. It is in these first days of spring that we see the ways in which simple beauty comforts and inspires. An awareness of the bounty of nature and its effect upon the home grows.

———————

"Outdoors we are confronted everywhere with wonders;
we see that the miraculous is not extraordinary,
but the common mode of existence. It is our daily bread."

–WENDELL BERRY

———————

Even in the promise of spring, there remains a looming threat of frost and snow, and copious amounts of mud. But the pristine abundance arriving upon the landscape dispels fears of a potential regression in the weather. Finally, spring has arrived. Slowly, surely, we begin to embark upon floral feasting.

Design

The bringing of fresh life into our homes announces the breaking of the floral fast. As nature awakens from hibernation, homes can also become filled with color and cheer. Few things compare with the newness of freshly cut bulb flower stems. This month varies from region to region, for some there is a reemergence of daffodils, tulips, and fritillaria. The season of camellias that carried us through winter winds down. The sight of new growth brings joy as the eye can see green buds forming on trees and shrubs.

"Awake, O north wind,
and come, O south wind!
Blow upon my garden."

—SONG OF SOLOMON 4:16

The architectural nature of branches, particularly those clipped with budding blooms, is a striking way of announcing spring's arrival in the home. Even those bare stems not yet ready to bloom add interest to any room and beautifully communicate the anticipation of the season. Cherry blossoms enchant the passersby whether still on the tree or tucked into a corner of the home. The beautiful simplicity of flowering branches in a vase recalls within the home the same wonder taking place outside.

The Basics of a Hand-Tied Bouquet

The ability to create a lush, hand-tied bouquet is a wonderful skill to possess. Making a gift of flowers to present to a hostess, a performer after a recital, or to a loved one "just because" is incredibly simple once we learn the mechanics of building the shape. The building of layers creates interest within the design and makes a home for each flower. This process is different from a bouquet held by an individual during a wedding or prom, as that would require other techniques to create a 360-degree design.

A helpful principle in design is to work in pairings and odd numbers, miming the casual manner of flowers growing in nature. Thinking of the flowers as groupings of twos, threes, and fives (and even a single large-headed bloom) is helpful during the placement of flowers to create this natural look. Placing the stems at varying heights also gives a natural garden finish.

There are several layers within any lush bouquet (which is not altogether different from creating an arrangement in a vase, but does have a few differences as you arrange while holding the flowers):

1. *Begin with a structural base of greenery*: Take a few stems of greenery, holding them in your hand to form a beginning shape. Often, the greenery will fall in such a way to dictate where the flowers should go. In the demonstration, I used two stems of seeded eucalyptus.

2. *The addition of textural and structural flowers*: Follow the shape established by the greenery to place flower stems that have a unique texture and structure. In the demonstration, I used two stems of button mums and three stems of sea holly thistle.

Often in this step, I utilize flowers that are branchy and have more than one flower on its stem.

3. *The addition of supporting flowers*: Supporting flowers are smaller headed blooms that act as a bridge between the structure and the focal point of the bouquet. I used medium sized mums.

4. *Intentionally place the focal flowers*: The placement of the focal flowers becomes more evident as the design progresses, most often to the front and center. Be sure to place the focal blooms in varying heights and locations, making use of the pairings principle to create a natural look. I utilized large headed spider mums.

5. *Completing the design with airy accents*: A lovely, lush garden is always complete with airy flowers that seem to dance in the wind above the other flowers in the garden. The addition of these flowers is what most sets the natural tone of the bouquet. Typically placed at a height above the other layers, but depending upon the flower, these can be tucked closer to the focal blooms. I use scabiosa and Queen Anne's Lace.

6. *Trim all the stems and bind them*: You'll want to make sure all the stems are the same length at the bottom and secure them with a rubber band to hold the flowers in place in the current shape. Secure it by taking three sturdy stems of the bouquet to anchor one end of the band, gently wrapping it around all the stems and securing it on a few sturdier, thicker stems—which is key—just beyond the first point of anchoring.

7. *Add some decorative final touches*: Complete the bouquet by wrapping it in kraft paper and finished it with ribbon or twine (a tutorial can be found on page "Wrapping Presentation Bouquets" on page 142).

Designing bouquets is one of the most enjoyable creative endeavors. The consideration of the mechanics eases the process. Repetition makes it intuitive, and the more you arrange, you will learn to see that the flowers will tell you where they want to go. Of course, improvisation and spontaneity are really at the heart of taking the beauty found outdoors and distilling it into a vase. However, having a general framework for a guideline permits newfound freedom in design.

SPRING

A feeling of solace is imparted upon the listener when hearing the first few notes of Antonio Vivaldi's "Spring" concerto from *The Four Seasons*. They are vigorous and bright, in stark contrast to the dissident and blustery sounds of the "Winter" concerto. These notes musically mirror what is taking place as the seasons change. Spring breathes an energetic sigh of relief, and in that sigh, life is brought forth in sprouts of green poking through the earth. The imagery of chirpy hatchlings also serves as a harbinger during this time of year, communicating the newness of life. In spring, hope abounds. Progress is now made manifest as we receive the first glimpses of life after a long, cold winter.

There is an undeniable charm to spring. A newfound sense of joy is present. Though quiet serenity is associated with winter, there is an undeniable peace found in the sounds of life that pierce the silence at the dawn of spring. Budding and blossoming branches fill the sky as buzzing insects, birdsong, and the patter of raindrops fill the air. The sun warms our chilled faces and fingers. What a mercy the season of spring is! After the quiet introspection of the winter, our posture changes—eases and softens, even—to begin again and rebloom alongside nature.

After a season mostly spent indoors staying warm, spring reconnects us with nature as our hands become dirty preparing the soil for planting. The

landscape dramatically changes in an instant. All that was quiet bursts forth into liveliness. Patience and anticipation still linger, as what has already been planted starts to grow, the warmer days of spring are still to come, and in some places, the ground is not yet ready for planting.

Flowers become a social occasion as floral arranging parties reemerge onto the social calendar scene like tulips bursting through the ground. It is in these moments gathered around long tables where laughter and blossoming beauty abound. Whether for a bridal or baby shower, girls' night out, or fun occasion with friends and children, creating alongside another instills a deeper appreciation for both person and flower. As we remember that both friendship and flowers nourish the soul, in the springtime, we find physical nourishment from flowers as we brew dandelion and clover

teas or consume cooked bright-orange zucchini flowers stuffed with soft cheeses and aromatic flavors. Gardens, and their bounties, are sources of joy and inspiration.

"For see, the winter is past. . . .
The flowers appear on the earth,
the time of pruning the vines has come,
and the song of the turtledove is heard in our land."

—SONG OF SONGS 2:11–12 NABRE

Spring is the season of nature's song—one of hyperbole—as life returns to the landscape, balanced by typically temperate weather. The days are longer and the nights continue to grow shorter. There is a chorus of birdsong at daybreak whose chirping melodies are as diverse as the flora awakening. It is in this consolation that we join in the refrain from the book of Daniel as he hearkens all of creation to "bless the Lord." These are joys made possible by the succession of blooms that spring from the thawing earth.

"For flowers that bloom about our feet;
For tender grass, so fresh so sweet;
For song of bird and hum of bee;
For all things fair we hear or see;
Father in heaven, we thank Thee!"

–RALPH WALDO EMERSON

Enduring Trials

It's easy to fall into despair and discouragement when our best intentions and well-laid plans lie in ruin, not just in gardening—where it is most tangibly apparent—but in countless other aspects of life. Disappointment is an unavoidable reality when things do not go as planned. Endless elements of life, from our vocations down to date nights and all that happens in between, can seemingly go belly-up with little redemption or recourse. Whether large or small events, these are often pivotal moments that force us to change our footing and pivot in another direction.

While preparing this book, a storm swept through the Deep South that unleashed tornadoes, damaging winds, and torrential rains. I looked out my bedroom window in terror as the ominous clouds rapidly approached, bringing with them a straight-line wind—trees cracked and uprooted and weightlessly crashed upon the ground and atop two recently planted flower beds. At that moment, my primordial instincts focused me on my family's safety. But when the winds subsided and all the damage was bare, I mourned the loss of my newly emerging flowers. Yet just as in life, goodness could emerge from the loss.

Out in our pasture just beyond our fence grew a mighty oak tree, covered with luscious purple wisteria vine that towered sixty feet above the ground. For years I had wanted to cut the lovely vines for an arrangement, but the branches and blooms were much too high to access. Now, however, those vines were strewn upon the ground, the storm having taken down the tree. An abundance of wisteria was now at my fingertips that I could not previously reach.

My new flower beds were still crushed, as was our fence. And pencils and notepads chronicling my thoughts for this book accrued dust as I redirected all efforts toward clean-up, assessment, and rebuilding. During this time, it became easy to discern the parallels between that moment of pivoting and balance of home life, professional life, and so much more. A fresh perspective is often born from the trial. All is transient. But the sun reemerges from the clouds. Amid trial, we sort through the mess, with our faces pointed toward God, relying ever more deeply upon His providence.

Often, beautiful outcomes are born from difficult moments, moments made possible by the forced pivot. Inventory is taken and reevaluated, and a new perspective is born. Unique and beautiful realities previously unavailable form before our eyes, like a wreath made from the wisteria vines growing on the oak tree.

April

Colors abound and warmth prevails as March rolls into April. This is the month in which we usually celebrate the Lord's resurrection. In my childhood, on Easter morning, upon crossing the threshold of the sanctuary, I would breathe as deeply as my lungs would permit to take in the wondrous scent filling the church. To me, the sweet perfume and lovely pastel shades of the hyacinth are synonymous with this most sacred of days. It is beautifully poetic that Our Lord resurrected in the springtime, as all of nature returns to life alongside its Savior.

Easter is such a joyous occasion that it is often celebrated in flowers. So, it seems only right that we take a piece of God's gloriously redeemed creation and make it the focal point of our Easter dinner tables. Fragrant and bright stems convene on the table, recalling Eden, but foremost the love of the New Adam and a Father who gave both Son and garden as everlasting gifts.

With most threats of snow passed, gardening can begin in earnest. Much needs to be done before a flower can emerge from the seed. Our toil, combined with the cooperation of rain and sun, work together to go into the beauty of a garden landscape. The fruits of labor are well worth the energy expended in the process.

The world begins to exhale, and that surge of air brings an awakening. April is a month of happy surprises. The scent of fresh dirt and fragrant blooms permeate the air as the previously planted flowers reemerge. Bulbs poke through the softening earth. Bleeding hearts return to the landscape with tender little blooms that hang like delicate jewelry. Lily of the valley, modestly tucked against the ground, easily overlooked, puts on a charming display alongside delicate and sweetly fragrant grape hyacinth. Azaleas show off their vibrant colors against the remaining bare branches of trees. Forsythia, with its small but intensely yellow blooms, set fire to the landscape. Wisteria vines soften the view with draping, grape-like flowers.

"Flowers are the music of the ground.
From earth's lips spoken without sound."

–EDWIN CURRAN

Flowering branches develop simple green leaves, which in turn cede the stage to the primroses growing beneath the canopy. In their purple richness, violets cheerfully bloom against the soil. Flowers increase with each passing day. Fragrant blooms have an immense association with the season as hyacinths, as well as other varieties of narcissus and fritillaria, perfume the air with their lovely aroma.

Tulips, like daffodils and many other bulb flowers, require a cold winter to ensure good flowering in the spring. The endless varieties of tulips range from complex layers of petals, varying shades within one flower, to other varieties with unexpected spiky edges. They are a flower in high demand, so much so that in fifteenth-century Holland, there was an economic market crash over tulips. The personality of this flower is perfectly captured in their droopy elegance by Dutch Master painters like Ambrosius Bosschaert the Elder.

The rain comes in April, bringing with it growth that needs to be tended. Nature brings rain as a remedy to nourish the earth like a mother tending to her child. Rainwater's nutrients are necessary in the feeding and development of foliage vital to the plant's survival. God's ordering of creation provides all that is needed at the right time. Clouds grumble as their growth produces friction between them. It is such a joyful time of year that even the rain clouds seem to console each other. In the rain, we witness the merging of sky and earth through little droplets of water.

"It's exciting to see things coming up again, plants that you've had for twenty or thirty years. It's like seeing an old friend."

—TASHA TUDOR

A rainy day at home brings a continuous and melodious sound, from soothing sounds of droplets hitting windowpanes to the familiar splashing sound of cars driving to the arias of birds thankful for the refreshment. Rain provides an opportunity to be present within the home while offering a break from some of the garden's toil.

There is something about the freshness of spring rain. It is so captivating that many companies attempt to mimic the aroma in their products. This natural perfume, known as petrichor, is the scent that comes from an oil excreted by plants during a dry spell that becomes fragrant upon the relief of the rain. Rain rewards the new growth and beckons its continuance.

Despite the joy found in water falling from the skies, it is foremost universally nourishing. All life on earth would perish without water. It is rain that provides nature's abundance, as it is the source of life with each hour of rain that passes, the greenness of the grass increases. It comes as no surprise, then, that in arid areas, one is hard-pressed to find life. Conversely, the species of flora are innumerable in the wet jungle.

"What a desolate place would be
a world without a flower."

–CLARA LUCAS BALFOUR

One of the many benefits of rain is that the effects are often immediate. Wilted or parched plants regain shape. The dancing, rippling effect of one drop of rain shows the life-giving potential of each droplet. Riverbeds and creeks rise. Like leaf pile jumping in the fall, wellies, umbrellas, and the exuberant puddle jumping of spring reside in a special place in childhood memories. In the absence of rain, we become acutely aware of our need. It is in times of drought, like a fast, when plants are dry and withered, that we are aware of the importance of this life-giving force.

It is often a mystery why the Christian life starts with water, until we recognize its vitality and necessity in nature. Of course, God would start with water. He always starts with water.

Spring affords an optimistic outlook even during rainstorms, as the dampness provides a bounty. In winter, we often forget the purpose of the cold, but during the spring, it is easy to remember the purpose of those rain-filled days. The rains of spring are hope-filled as they bring sustenance to our new

flower friends popping up all over. The importance of perspective cannot be understated in life. Just as we spiritually need the cleansing waters of baptism to wash our parched souls, the growing flowers also need water. We see, in flowers, precisely why we need the rain. As the character Eponine sings in *Les Miserables*: the "rain will make the flowers grow."

Very little of nature seems to remain in slumber between fauna and flora, and the atmosphere enveloping them. The warmth of April days facilitates the rejuvenation of the garden as its rain nourishes the tender, new growth. It is the near memory of the cold and barren winter days that aids our gratitude in April.

Design

The first full month of spring is one of immense bulb flowers. April is when I feel most inspired to recreate Dutch Master paintings filled with interesting flowers like tulips and fritillarias. Drooping flowers over urns are a wonderfully dramatic backdrop mimicking the new drama of the garden. The simple placement of tulips into a goblet cup or a vase filled with fragrant lilac can enliven an entire room. Such easy arrangements can still carry an immense impact. Many ferns and other greenery have fully come into their own during April. An arrangement of mixed foliage is both interesting and long-lasting and serves as a great celebration of the greening of the outdoors. Nostalgically potted plants in colorful foil make their way home at Eastertime containing either hyacinth, Easter lilies, tulips, or daffodils. Once their blooming has ended, plant them into the ground so that you may enjoy them again the following year.

"When the sweet showers of April have pierced
the drought of March, and pierced it to the root,
and every vein is bathed in that moisture whose
quickening force will engender the flower;
and when the west wind too with its sweet breath
has given life in every wood and field."

—GEOFFREY CHAUCER

The Language of Flowers

Flowers communicate an unspoken language. The symbolism behind each flower ranges from culture to culture, from century to century. In Victorian times, flowers conveyed a great deal to the receiver, particularly during a time in which it was deemed proper etiquette to repress emotions. To receive hot house roses during the Georgian period was most certainly something to swoon over and something befitting of a Jane Austen novel. However, a flower of the narcissus variety communicated egotism and was decidedly not swoony, regardless of where it was grown.

Flower color also sent a message. A rose, for example, speaks to love, but it can also have many meanings, depending upon the shade: a white rose means "purity and spiritual love"; a yellow rose means a "decrease of love and infidelity." Where a cabbage rose was an "ambassador of love," a single rose told of simplicity. Catholics are very aware of the symbolism of the lily as purity, often used in renderings of saints. In modernity, the meaning of flowers is more inconsequential. Nonetheless, I have had the experience of taking orders from foreign clients forbidding certain flowers because of what they would communicate.

Flowers communicate what often isn't said, and are a big part of our spoken language as well. To "stop and smell the roses" is to pause, slow down the hectic life, and take in what is before us. "Coming up roses" means that things are going well. "Ups a daisy" is commonly used as we rise after falling. No western is complete without a threat that a sworn enemy will be "pushing daisies." And to "nip in the bud" signifies an ending of something in its early stages.

It is lovely to ponder the dichotomy of the language of flowers—namely, the consequences of what they convey in the unspoken word contrasted to the explicitness of an idiom. Also fascinating is the messages that what flowers express has changed throughout time and varies between cultures. It is in this relationship between flowers and communication that we recognize their deep-seated cultural reality.

May

Wild roses blossom within an untamed landscape as bees make a triumphant return, dancing from blossom to bloom in May. The sun climbs higher as the season progresses and freshly mowed grass whispers to our sense of smell. May is the preeminent month for flowers as new varieties make their debut, bursting forth in vibrant colors. There is much to take in as the landscape teems with flowers.

Roses engage the senses. The beauty of these diverse flowers is unending. Roses have been an enduring favorite throughout time. Never quite in vogue nor ever out of style, they represent the epitome of staying power. These flowers contain complex layers of beauty due to their richness of color, perfume, and shape. They are highly protected and guarded, as made evident by the rows of thorns below the enchanting flower head. The rose is a flower that you discover more deeply once you think you know all there is to know. It is no wonder why many have dedicated their lives' work to these flowers.

Prairie roses are a charming, unbridled relative of standard roses that ramble and grow at will. With the help of birds spreading their seeds, they grow in a less controlled fashion than cultivated and bred roses. Even in their unpolished temperament, prairie roses are a constant source of charm. Since roses are one of the oldest plants to be cultivated, with fossils found dating back thirty-five million years, it comes as no surprise that they are still such a prominent flower. The lovely scent of roses is often replicated in perfumes and soaps. One of the most wonderful aspects of roses is the light floral flavor of the petals. A late afternoon May beverage of rose petals infused water with lemon and basil is a wonderfully refreshing way to enjoy the complexity of their beauty.

"The splendor of the rose and the whiteness of the lily
do not rob the little violet of its scent
nor the daisy of its simple charm.
If every tiny flower wanted to be a rose,
spring would lose its loveliness."

—SAINT THÉRÈSE OF LISIEUX

Though roses may have captured the hearts of many through the centuries, other May flowers are equally wondrous to enjoy. Foxgloves are blooming contradictions as they are both humble cottage flowers but also majestic in their tall spires and delicate bell-like petals. With the help of a busy army of ants, tight peony buds burst open to reveal one of the most impressive blooms. Annual seeds purchased and collected begin to go into the steadily warming soil. Popping up in the middle of garden beds, phlox are a fantastic filler in both borders and vases. Tiny flowers on strawberry plants give way to edible buds. All feels hopeful in the unfurling of the variance of flowers of May.

Saint Anselm of Canterbury once said, "He who could create all things from nothing would not remake His ruined creation without Mary. God,

then, is the Father of the created world and Mary, the mother of the re-
created world." In springtime, the world is anew. It is only fitting that during
this resurgence of life, Our Lady is, in some measure, a part. No Catholic floral book worth its salt would allow the month of Mary to pass without men-
tioning the cause of so much floral wonder. It is a blessing that God made the
world a garden for us, His children. It should only seem appropriate that He
should inspire the love of the Mother of God in a floral way.

There is no more fitting month to venerate the Mother of God than in
May, as creation is fully reborn. I imagine each of God's children to be the
unique flower called to mind by the epigraph at the start of this chapter,
inspiring words that come to us from Saint Thérèse of Lisieux. Everyone's

beauty and individual gifts combine to form a wondrous landscape. Each flower reflects the reality of the soul; it is not merely a copy but a singular creation. No two are the same. A specific work of art, no matter how affecting it may be, loses its shine upon familiarity. It is not so with the presentation of each new flower; each has singular characteristics that distinctively fill a field of flowers.

A walk on a garden path in the warm May sunshine can offer dozens of reminders of Our Lady as iris stems bloom and their petals create a fleur-de-lis shape, recalling the French symbol for Mary. This humble woman has been the center of the floral world for centuries. Saint Bede articulated one of the loveliest descriptions of the Blessed Mother when he stated that not only does the lily call to mind her purity but the golden anthers represent the beauty of her soul.

"The rose of charity, the lily of chastity,
the violet of humility and the
golden gillyflower of heaven."

—SAINT BERNARD SPEAKING OF THE BLESSED VIRGIN MARY

Over the centuries, many flowers have been named in honor of Mary or have become synonymous with her in some other manner. In many cases, these flowers once bore the title of "Our Lady" before it: Our Lady's Mantle, Our Lady's Thistle, and even foxglove was once known as Our Lady's Glove. Of course, Mary's Gold is now affectionately called Marigold. Floral imagery is beautifully woven into the Litany of the Blessed Virgin Mary as we implore her intercession as the "Mystical Rose." Saint John

Henry Newman stated that Mary "is the Queen of spiritual flowers; and therefore she is called the Rose, for the rose is fitly called of all flowers the most beautiful."

"We never give more honour to Jesus than
when we honour his Mother, and we honour her simply
and solely to honour him all the more perfectly.
We go to her only as a way leading to the
goal we seek—Jesus, her Son."

—SAINT LOUIS DE MONTFORT

Mary is like a loving pollen bee drifting between flowers, taking along a little piece of pollen from each to nurture and grow an entire garden, eventually creating a sweet honey from the pollen collection. This imagery calls to mind the power of her intercessory role in the Church. Mary, the new Eve, tends to the garden of souls entrusted to her by Our Lord from the cross. There is no more perfect help for these precious and delicate souls than the one who nurtured and raised the world's Savior. As the gaze of the flowers is upon the sun, the little bee does humble, hidden, and vital work with the flowers she so gently encounters. A mother works similarly, unnoticed in the backdrop of the home, just as the bee also quietly maintains the garden's life. The work of Our Lady is discreet, as seen during her quiet imploration of Christ at the wedding feast at Cana and her first Christ-bearing work of evangelization at the Visitation.

Much can be learned by meditating on the lifespan of a flower. It unfolds as its countenance faces the sun. Its head turns out of necessity, reaching toward the sunlight, its source of life, with total dependence. As we permit our petals to open, we open ourselves to our fullest potential while also benefiting life all around. As countless flowers unfurl to display their beauty during the month of May, the opportunities for this type of meditation are as numerous as the flowers that bloom.

"The bee is more honored than other animals,
not because she labors, but because
she labors for others."

—SAINT JOHN CHRYSOSTOM

Design

Floral design in May is almost endless with possibility. Commonly loved available flowers include peonies, roses, irises, phlox, prairie roses, foxgloves, sweet peas, snapdragons, and so much more. Such variety allows for any number of exciting arrangements. Forms of shapes, textures, and sizes play with and against each other, highlighting the diversity of flora. You can use the

edibles from the kitchen garden (or market) to create an excellent design by tucking in fragrant herbs or budding strawberry stems. Dogwood trees come alive with their distinguished flowers and are a perfect structural piece to add. In mid- to late-spring, it is still cool enough that countless types of ferns are available to use as attractive foliage in a design.

The Basics of an Arrangement

Floral design is an ancient art. Countless design styles have existed throughout time, but the most striking arrangements are those that imitate the lines of nature. Similar to most art and fashion, floristry trends ebb and flow. Some styles, however, withstand the test of time. There have been times when very ordered, upright designs have been in vogue, but I am partial to the current trends of loose designs coined by the phrase "garden designs."

In this style, arrangements convey the imagery of a garden with delicate and diverse detail. Seldom are gardens visually one dimension but rather contain all manners of variance in height. Varying textures and colors can add depth and interest to a design, and a simple arrangement with one type of flower also has its charms. But the way in which the flowers (whether diverse in number or simple) live in the vase create the interest in the design. Regardless of the ingredients, floral designs are most striking when the stems are allowed to graze and fall over the edge of the container so that the lines of the flower and vase blend to become one entity. The principles of layering elements are akin to making a bouquet, but the execution is different.

The following steps create a lush, garden style arrangement that can be universally applied to any container:

1. *Foundations:* The foundation of creating an arrangement lies in where the flowers will be placed. Deciding which flowers to use will determine the composition of the arrangement, as well as what container to be used. Will it be a centerpiece for a table? Will it be on a prominent table in the center of a room, or will it be tucked against a wall? Is it

a little arrangement that will sit on a bathroom sink? These answers will determine the height, width, and placement of flowers (for example, flower arrangements against a wall do not require the same 360-degree placement of flowers like a table centerpiece).

2. *Choose and prepare the vessel:* If it is wide-mouthed, secure it with a frog or balled up chicken wire (or both). Fill the container with water, at least a fingertip's distance to the lip of the container.

3. *Determining flower amount:* Knowing the size of the vessel will help determine the number of flowers needed to complete the arrangement. Bud vases require very little flowers, whereas urns require many flowers to complete.

4. *Building the main structure:* Greenery is arguably the most important part of the process. It is what gives the arrangement its lush appearance, physically supports the flowers to remain in place, and helps to lessen the number of flowers needed to complete the design. Using greenery, build the base structure of the arrangement at varying heights and angles. Take cues from the asymmetrical beauty of the garden (examples: evergreens, boxwood, laurel, ninebark, pittosporum, begonias, dusty miller, eucalyptus, bay leaf, and more). Add personality to the structure with branchy, filler flowers that help with establishing structure and personality (examples: euphorbias, bupleurum, honey wort, lady's mantle, spray roses, and much more). Pro tip: it is important to cut stems at a 45-degree angle to ensure their ability to take in water within the vase. A flat-bottomed stem can end

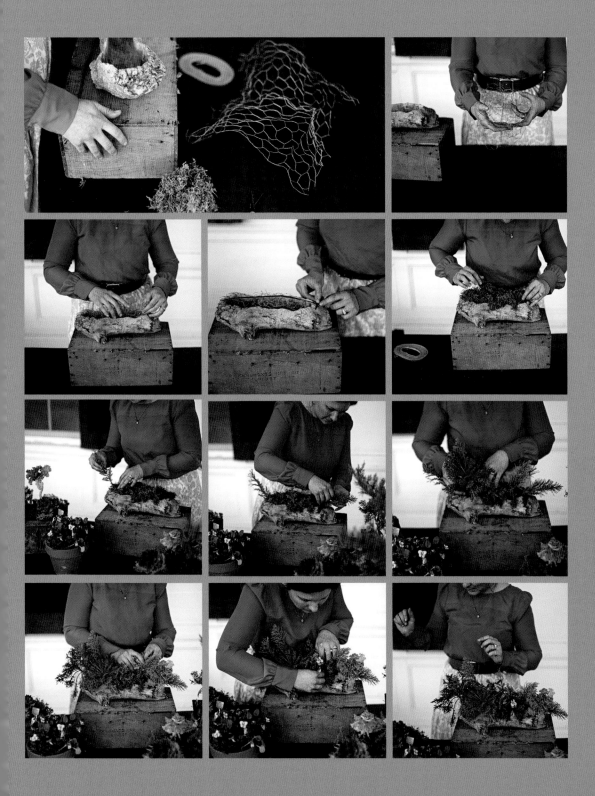

up on the bottom of the container and be unable to drink water.

5. *Building out the arrangement:* Once the structure is established, create interest with textural elements placed in the open spaces (examples: honeysuckle, love in a puff, ferns, and much more).

   Pro tip: Make sure that no leaves fall below the water line of the arrangement. This leads to a buildup of bacteria that will shorten the vase life of the flowers.

6. *Layering with supporting flowers:* Add supporting flowers throughout the arrangement in the holes not filled in by other steps. These are beautiful flowers that create a home for focal flowers to stand out. Their blooms tend to be smaller-headed (examples: yarrow, gomphrena, foxglove).

   Pro tip: If the arrangement is going to be placed up against a wall, the arrangement will only need to be one-sided, so no need to put flowers on the backside.

7. *Completing the arrangement:* Now, the greatest fun begins with adding focal flowers and airy accents. Placing at varying heights creates a layered and natural look, like the appearance of flowers growing in a garden. Place the focal blooms in places of prominence. Focal blooms tend to be large-headed flowers (peonies, roses, hydrangeas, lilies, dahlias, and many more).

   Pro tip: it's best to begin estimating the placement in the arrangement with longer stems and trim them down slowly to the right height. Once a flower is cut too short, the stem won't regrow (unless it's a tulip!). Complete the story with the delicate accents, either dancing above the arrangement or gently beneath and around the focal flowers (examples: Queen Anne's lace, feverfew, fritillaria, grasses, and many more). These same principles are universally applicable to various containers.

8. *Extending the life of the arrangement:* There are many tips and tricks to ensuring an extended life of an arrangement, but few are as simple and as effective as simply changing the water once it becomes visibly cloudy, and giving the stems a fresh cut after changing the water.

9. *Cleaning up:* Be sure to wash your containers with dish soap and water after each use!

June

In June, a sea of tall spires of hollyhock and delphinium reach toward heaven, while allium, bergamot, and poppies curtsy in the wind. The harmonies between floral solos blend into a visual symphony. Bergamot, affectionately known as bee balm, grows wild, spreading as far as it can reach its lavender blooms. Its magnetism for pollinators and endless charm as a cut flower make it a welcome late spring or early summer friend. Full billowing vines of clematis creep their way to the top of trellises. Gigantic magnolia flowers cover waxy green trees. Campanulas are akin to foxglove in their bell-shaped petals but are happy to keep their gaze upon the ground. Eclectic sea hollies, with their blue-spiked petals, entertain the eyes. Firework-like and cheery, crocosmia celebrates the warmer days that have come.

Time seems to pause in June, yet flowers maintain a monthly and hourly rhythm. That they keep a schedule is made evident by flowers that bloom only when the sun shines, like the morning glory, or those that emit a fragrance only in the evening, like star jasmine. In this way, a garden permits room for anticipation as we learn the unique tendencies of each flower.

Humanity's story began in a garden, crafted from the soil. Our reconciliation to the Father commenced in the garden of Gethsemane with the new Adam. Perhaps, therefore, we find a particular purpose when tending to flowers as our journeys are intertwined. Placing our hands into the soil to plant the garden and arranging with cut stems acknowledges this foundation. A garden is a "where," a backdrop for an encounter, and not so much a "what" or thing. It is a place to enjoy and cultivate while God forms us.

"If you look the right way,
you can see that the whole world is a garden."

—FRANCIS HODGSON BURNETT

The garden is a space where nature and man collide and cooperate. As we meander along a pathway in a well-loved garden, we witness this beautiful unity. In gardening, the gardener seeks to highlight the marvelousness of creation, not subdue it. The plants, when lovingly tended, follow the gardener's direction. Yet despite the cooperation, the elements are dominant and unpredictable due to weather patterns making or breaking a season. Soggy rains bring rot, drought withers the plant. Blight and pests are challenges too, bringing about a different pathway toward a new equilibrium between the gardener and creation. Even still, in the encounter with the garden, we recognize the beauty and its attainable joy because of the importance of God's created order and the complex relationship between feast and fast. Gardening challenges our self-reliance, which stands in the way of God. We must be sure

to only rely upon providence as things can still go wrong, despite our best efforts.

Throughout the year, a garden evolves and requires varying amounts of attention. In June, the work crescendos. Planting and watering are among the most favorable tasks, weeding, the most necessary of all jobs, lest the garden goes to ruin. The gardener's work is never complete. Life never stops providing opportunities to gain experience and learn. A gardener must never rest on her laurels, for weeds' growth can quickly destroy a garden's beauty.

Pulling the tiny weeds that grew between the bricks of the front walkway was my least favorite chore during childhood. My fingers bled from the continual friction against the brick. To a twelve-year-old, it was hard to understand the purpose of this task. The little weeds seemed less problematic than sore fingers. Yet removing these weeds was vital; their absence made the pathway to the front door more welcoming.

In the garden, there exists constant competition between weeds and plants. Weeds are a nutritional detriment as they battle plants for access to the necessary components for survival: sunlight and water. Their dominance inevitably weakens the plant. Certain weeds impose a threat to the gardener, like poison ivy. As weeds overtake a garden, the beauty of the flowers diminish not only because they compete for nutrients and light but also because they are a distraction. Analogously, weeds are akin to vices overshadowing virtue. Often beginning small and harmlessly, they grow wildly when uncontrolled. Even though some sins are more toxic than others, all seek to ruin the harmony between our virtues. An unknown author stated, "The difference between a flower and a weed is a judgment." There is immense importance in prayerful discernment to identify and root out the weeds that corrupt the good that God wants to cultivate in us. Vice and weeds often present themselves gently and appealingly, only to become detrimental to the good, and difficult to root out once established. There is a reward to persevering through weeding in both the spiritual and gardening life. The formerly hidden beauty can shine. The complementary aspects of the good within are once more apparent.

"So neither he who plants nor he who waters
is anything, but only God who gives the growth."

—1 CORINTHIANS 3:7

A balance must exist in the pursuit of rooting out weeds and not accidentally rooting out flowers. Many master gardeners insist on increasing the planting density to aid in the prohibition of weed growth. This approach has a pearl of overarching wisdom, as planting more virtue makes it more difficult for vice to creep in and establish—the more one weeds and feels "on top of things," the more manageable the work. A well-tended and maintained garden brings ease, as with our souls. We must remove the entire weed to access

the soil to plant seeds. If troublesome weeds return, the gardener finds herself constantly battling the same issue and lacking the space to produce the beautiful flowers that make a garden.

"Gardening is the work of a lifetime: you never finish."

—OSCAR DE LA RENTA

The task of weeding, though not enjoyable, is enormously rewarding. It requires a great deal of humility to lower oneself close to the soil—or in Latin, *humus*, the root word for humility—to better identify weeds from

flowers threatening the garden's beauty and work to prevent future incursions. Likewise, staking weak or injured blooms requires a meek touch. As in life, we are better able to access our faults and be a help to others while in a posture of humility.

"In all things of nature,
there is something of the marvelous."

−ARISTOTLE

The delightful resurgence of birdsong, the hum of bugs, the flash of fireflies, and the ribbet of frogs return at spring's end. Like March, June is another month containing two seasons. Yet it has a very subtle way of welcoming summer. Gentle increases in temperature give heed to the sun's proximity. Amid the toil, it is good to pause and take in the beauty of spring blending into summer. Time in the garden puts life into perspective with the rhythm of creation ever before us. Gardening reflects the fragility of life, a reality most evident in the busiest month in the garden. There will always be failures and losses, but also triumphs and growth. It is in the work and the risk that we find gain and reward. Gardens and flowers evolve through the month, the year, and over the years, as do we.

Design

As the calendar year begins to crescendo over the next few weeks, the gathering and arranging of flowers becomes increasingly simple. It is fun to arrange in a way that translates the landscape into a vase. The easiest way of doing this is by accumulating a lovely handful of stems with abandon, trimming the bottoms to the same length, and placing them into a vase. June is a simple month, and so can our arrangements be. Effortless beauty is enough; all that is required is to enjoy.

Getting the Most Out of Your Flowers

Working with flowers is a joy whether you arrange them with homegrown stems or sourced from a flower shop or supermarket. Relish your design for days by taking specific steps to extend their vase life. If you have had enough exposure to the flower world, you have probably heard the term "conditioning." Conditioning flowers is the care taken after harvesting to increase their longevity. If you purchase cut flowers, it is also helpful to know what to seek and avoid when choosing stems to ensure you can enjoy your arrangement for as long as possible.

Tips for conditioning flowers after cutting them at home:

- It is best to harvest flowers in the morning before the heat of the day sets in or in the evening after it has passed.

- Once flowers have been cut on an angle and lower leaves removed, place them into a bucket or vase with fresh room temperature water and allow them to rest and have a good drink for an hour or so.

Most flowers are happy with this conditioning method. However, there are certain flowers that require a different process to be properly conditioned.

- Woody flower stems like hydrangea or lilacs benefit from an additional vertical slit up from the base of the stem about two inches.

- Flowers that excrete a milky sap upon cutting, like euphorbia, poinsettia, or milkweed, can be dipped into hot water for fifteen to twenty seconds to stop the sap.

- Daffodils need to condition in their own container for an hour after being harvested and before being mixed with other flowers.

- Flowers that have become droopy after harvesting can be revived by being straightened and wrapped in newspaper to keep them upright, and then given a fresh cut and placed back into water to rehydrate.

Tips for looking for the freshest cut flowers when purchasing:

- One of the keys to successful flower buying is to seek the freshest flowers possible. The appearance and feel of the flowers will show the freshness.

- Inspect the petals and leaves of the flower to make sure they aren't discolored with black spots or are visibly wilting.

- Flower petals that are still close to bud form (for varieties like peonies) will last longer since they haven't fully bloomed yet, and will open over the next day or two.

- To ascertain the freshness of a rose, you will need to gently squeeze the head; it should be on the firmer side. If it is soft, it isn't as fresh.

Some tips to prolong the life of your floral arrangement:

- Always make sure the water in your vase is clear and clean. Once it becomes cloudy, change the water out and give the stems a fresh cut.

- Double check that no leaves are submerged in water. Remove any that are below the water line to prevent bacteria growth.

- Keep the arrangement away from windows or heat sources.

- Always be sure to use clean vases.

- Lastly, make sure that the water is topped off in the vase so that all the stem bottoms are in water.

SUMMER

The sun illuminates the world in a golden hue during the summertime. The landscape becomes a floral retreat. Humid days cause the lush meadows to have a painted appearance. There is adventure, wonder, imagination. Nature contains so much promise. Our gardens take on a meadow-like appearance as wildflowers spill out beyond garden beds. Summertime exists in an abundance of categorically common flowers, but the bulk of them, like Queen Anne's lace, create a sensation. Though life's activities slow during the next few months, the gardener's work increases with vigor and speed. The air is hot and brimming with all forms of creatures in flight. Moments of a relieving breeze are welcome beyond measure. Birds endlessly compete with their solos and make momentary debuts from lovingly placed birdhouses to say hello.

The garden serves as a beautiful backdrop in all of life's dynamics. Gardens in the summertime become the lush place where people gather and are simply present, much like around a Christmas tree. We connect with each other and nature as we sit along tables brimming with food, elbows, and flowers under summer's star-speckled sky.

It is a season of extremes situated between temperate seasons, like winter. Winter's fast contrasts the feast of summer. Nature's generosity manifests its glory beneath the illumination of the sun. The dedication of waiting through the winter season and the toils of spring are rewarded as a sea of bounteous

blooms charms as far as the eye can see. Our senses are in overdrive. There is so much to perceive, to behold, to enjoy. Our ears listen to the chirping and buzzing, our feet feel the soft grasses underfoot. We inhale the floral fragrances dancing in the air. The sun warms the earth, and all contained within bursts open with color and fragrance in thanksgiving. Summertime mimics the spiritual reality of consolation, vitality, and abundance.

_____

"The earth laughs in flowers."

–RALPH WALDO EMERSON

_____

In the iconic 1972 hit "Summer Breeze," Seals and Crofts wonderfully encapsulated the wonder and joy of the ordinary things of summertime: open windows allowing the wind to move the curtains, fragrant jasmine perfuming the air, music dancing out of the next-door windows to serenade the passersby. The small pleasures of summer contain simple joy and combine to illustrate a culture in which a slow and present attentiveness rules the day. The famous George Gershwin ballad rightly declares, "summertime and the livin's easy." Such songs brilliantly put to melody what sets these three months apart: a posture of relaxation and receptivity, of consolation in the abundance. Leisure maintains a place of prominence as freedom and slowness are savored in preparation for busier times.

There is a deep connection between memory and scent. The aromatic summertime air is teaming with childhood memories. The sweet smell of honeysuckle reminds my mother of the freedom of play-filled days with friends. Joyful recollections of traipsing past large honeysuckle vines in neighbors' backyards flood her memory. To her, the smell overflows with joy. With happy memories, peace always envelops us.

Competing with the trills of the birds is the unmistakable crack of baseballs connecting with swinging bats. The abundant flowers of the garden frame the lemonade stand, a beacon of the nostalgic tenderness of summertime. The unhurried culture enables an attentive posture to observe the season's unique sounds and sights. The individual attention we give to each new bloom of spring changes into the greeting of an audience as summer's floral crowds makes for a grand show; a blooming exhibition in the garden that mirrors the intensity of the hot air with its luscious blooms and vibrant colors.

Wrapping Presentation Bouquets

Flowers are an enduringly popular hostess gift. No matter where they come from, whether from the garden, supermarket, or corner shop, a lovely bouquet is always fun to present and to receive. When I have given bouquets, I have noticed the posture of the recipients change, and their face lightens. Their entire countenances alter for the better. The opportunity to provide this joy for another is a gift in and of itself.

When gifting someone flowers, consider the following advice:

- A few simple tricks in presentation can make for a fun bouquet-giving experience. All it takes is craft paper and twine, and a hand-tied bouquet.

- After the bouquet has been arranged and tied off, begin to shape the kraft paper by folding it in half on an angle to create triangles.

- With the points of the paper facing upward, place the bouquet into the center of the triangle.

- Wrap the paper around one half at a time, with one side overlapping the other.

- Create a pinch point three-fourths of the way down the bouquet and secure it with twine or ribbon to tie into a bow at that pinch point.

Having this arrow in your quiver will give you immense confidence any time the need for a bouquet arises. Long gone are the days of rushing about to find a hostess gift or bouquet to present after a recital. It is a wonderful gift to give freshly cut flowers lovingly arranged by your hands.

July

Gardens seem to boast in July, the summertime's height, and the year's halfway point. It is easy to comprehend the etymology of the phrase "to flourish" during midsummer. The endless sea of flowers is reminiscent of the stars. All of nature seems to assume a posture of praise. Textured wildflowers of all shapes and sizes fill the vista as far as the eye can see. Dainty butterflies float from butterfly bush to milkweed and all the flowers in between. Tall branches of feathery celosia overshadow cheerful coneflowers, and black-eyed Susans add a vibrant color to the garden. We even admire the lovely strangers whose names we have not yet learned. Lilies of countless varieties spring forth from the warm ground, opening wide their star-like petals to say hello today. Though there are endless flowers to admire, the zinnia is the star of July: delicate in its varying shades and petal shape, humble in its simplicity, yet immensely hardy, easy to grow, and fun to arrange.

Annuals, like honeywort, sweet peas, and sunflowers, are a delight and make for wonderful cutting flowers. Their ability to fully mature from seed to colorful splendor over several weeks helps to quickly fill both garden beds and vases. Marigolds, nasturtium, and various herbaceous plants make their way into vases throughout the kitchen; their unique, aromatic personalities announce the height of the season.

July is the month of flower cutting and arranging in the fever pitch of abundance. Much of what we create lasts for a moment: a lovely meal, the perfect hairstyle, a clean kitchen. It is what happens in that moment of enjoyment that counts. The meal ends, the arrangements wilts, and still we create anew. Beauty is never a waste. As we arrange flowers, we arrange the sacred. We work with the marvels of God's creation; placing flowers in a vase is the simplest way to share these gifts' wonder. The world—and the home—are made more beautiful where their presence is welcomed.

———

"Are not flowers the stars of the earth?"

—CLARA LUCAS BALFOUR

———

Incorporating flowers in our home life need not be reserved for dinner parties and special guests. Being intentional about cultivating beauty in our homes speaks to the great dignity of home and its inhabitants. We are intentional not just for the building but for those within it to communicate love. When we give our very best, we make an act of love, serving intimately. As we work to nourish, shelter, and clothe, we should lavish those in our midst with the created beauty from our hands. Creating is an act of not only love but also thanksgiving for the One who is love and beauty.

Beauty affects our prayer life as it draws us into seeking God, who is beauty intangible. The more exposed we are to beauty and cooperation with God's creation, the more sensitive we are to Him. Using these gifts as a method of praise, we present our multiplied talents back to the Father, the fount of all blessings. There is more to flowers than meets the eye: they are prayer tools. To create is a form of prayer that mimics the work of God. God has allowed us to create, to share in His creation.

"Ora et Labora" lies at the heart of the Benedictine Order, where work and prayer are conjoined. Creating and cultivating beauty is work and another form of worship uniting hearts with God, not just in word but in action. In this way, floral design is a mode of meditation. This form of prayer within the domestic church fills the spaces of our hearts and homes in a new way as it unlocks a unique pathway toward the Creator. As we arrange each flower into an arrangement, we gather prayers and sacred gifts to elevate the home. Floral arrangements bridge our homes to the garden where we can walk with the Lord.

God is ever-present in nature. We commune with Him there. Jesus often retreated into the wilderness to be nearer to the Father as He prayed. In Gethsemane, Jesus sought to be nearer to the Father. He often united Himself to God through prayer in wild, vast, and uncultivated gardens.

"I do not think I have ever seen anything more beautiful than the bluebell I have been looking at. I know the beauty of our Lord by it."

—GERARD MANLEY HOPKINS

Our example of being ready to receive and to perceive the beauty around us helps to foster that quality in our children. Simple cut flowers are one of the more accessible ways to do this. Art can be expensive. Painting can feel overwhelming. But the extraordinary simplicity in a single flower's beauty rivals other ways we can impart beauty within the home. Flowers from your garden or purchased at a market facilitate this wonder. We go to great lengths to bring beauty into our lives with never-ending internet and magazine searches that create an insatiable desire. Yet, a single rose in a vase can transform not only a room but our perspective and priorities. In the face of distraction, it is easy to forget that the simplest, most accessible form of beauty is right at our fingertips, one that is both effortless and endless. So much in life cannot be controlled, but what we can do is make a beautiful space within which to take refuge and bring within that effortless and naturally occurring beauty.

"The power of finding beauty
in the humblest things
make home happy and life lovely."
–LOUISA MAY ALCOTT

Floral design is nature distilled into a vase. It is an imaginative work that speaks to the beauty of the landscape from which the flowers came, an intrinsic good that enables exploration and contemplation of the reality of the created world. Most of all, it is storytelling. It is the telling of a subtle story

reminding us that all beauty is a gift. The contemplation of each flower's ability to tell time through the calendar year and the course of human history shows us where we have been and where we are going, showcasing the tangible reality of God's faithfulness and provision.

"The ordinary arts we practice daily at home
are of more importance to the soul
than their simplicity might suggest."

–THOMAS MOORE

Design

Possibilities for floral arrangements are endless for designs in July. It would be easier to provide a list of flowers not in season, as the list of what is available could fill pages! A prayerful homage can be made to God's creation in the summertime by designing an arrangement that mimics untamed wildflower meadows. The designs can be complex, with multiple varieties of flowers or a simple monochromatic design of one kind of bloom. Wild bunches delight any container they call home.

Arranging the Unexpected

We can expand the types of designs we create by broadening our ingredients. Fruit and flowers are evocative of a still life Dutch Master painting. It is striking to see the fruit of the earth—edible and floral—side by side in an arrangement. Though it may seem initially odd, there is nothing lovelier than a stem of berries tucked alongside a fragrant rose. The sweetness they both provide is an artful display of nature at its best. In a dinner table centerpiece, the marriage between food and flower in a vase seems like an obvious winner. The contrast of texture is a feast for the eyes.

Edible additions to floral design will change depending upon the season. The visual of vegetables with bulb flowers in spring arrangements is a spectacular sight. I love the use of darling artichokes, spires of asparagus stalks, and heads of lettuce amongst the delicate spring flowers. In a season that imbues a feeling of a Beatrix Potter painting, it only seems appropriate that the tablescape should also appeal to dear Peter Rabbit or Jemima Puddleduck. In the summertime, adding unexpected branches of a tomato plant, berry plant, or fig tree is excellent, giving the nod to the beautiful abundance found outside. Of course, stalks of grains, bunches of grapes, and pumpkins can be arranged with flowers in autumn to mimic the atmosphere of the harvest. Kumquats, oranges, lemons, limes, and pomegranate add a splash of unique color and scent as well as beautiful dimension in the wintertime. Some produce sections make available many choices—from herbs to food on the vine. Fruit can be pierced with a wooden skewer and placed as a focal point within the arrangement.

Creating unique flower arrangements by celebrating all the garden's bounty opens creative avenues for design experimentation you never thought possible. You will never look at a stem of kale the same way again!

August

All that was vigorous in July tires as the calendar turns to August. Crickets and frogs are the great serenaders of the night when the blazing sun takes its rest. Malaise sets in, not just for the garden but for the gardener. Rocking chairs beneath covered porches become places of retreat from the scorching sun. It is in the dog days of summer when we cannot avoid the weight of the heat. We slow in the garden toil to rest as the heat incessantly overwhelms the outdoors. Gallant roses bloom despite the intensity of the heat, though the leaves are tired and thin. Yet the littlest mushrooms growing underfoot become apparent in the slight wilting of the landscape.

As we squeeze in summer travels before the school year begins, it is no surprise that the work of the garden has moved to the back burner. August is a month juxtaposed between busy times: planting and harvest. It is often the month of vacation. Once more, the providential ordering of the seasons provides much-needed opportunities for conserving energy due to the forces of nature. In the garden, it is in August that much goes to pot, as it is seldom a time of planting and often one of deferred maintenance. The heat causes plants to bolt and go to seed. Even though we slow our outdoor work, it does not stop the bounteous blooms that dahlias bring because of their striking color and form. The extensive vase life makes them an ideal cut flower.

Freshly cut dahlia stems smell of summer and signal the calendar's peak and the beginning of the slow descent to year's end.

———————

"There is nothing I like better at the end of a hot summer's day than taking a short walk around the garden. You can smell the heat coming up from the earth to meet the night air."

—PETER MAYLE

———————

We encounter a variation of flowers amidst our travels. As the odometer steadily increases, fields of golden corn and wheat awaiting harvest skirted by wildflowers witness our procession. It is extraordinary that flowers exist everywhere, from the oceans to the tops of mountains and the valleys and plains in between. No matter where we go, flowers are there to greet us. In France, open-air flower markets greet travelers with countless rows of buckets of fragrant flowers. Overabundant flowering shrubs climb over walls to say hello to the passersby in Spain. Hauntingly beautiful Spanish Moss hangs from trees in the southern United States, raising the curiosity as to whether an eccentric Flannery O'Connor character will appear at the next turn. Vibrant orange poppies bloom against the mountainous landscape in California, beckoning the onlooker to draw near. Japanese cherry blossoms stop awe-filled visitors in their tracks. An abundance of colorful, unique plants charm tropical vacationers. Flowers almost impossibly poke through the sandy earth of the coastline. In these moments, we see that flowers have been lovingly placed on the four corners of the globe and await us with anticipatory and joyful hospitality.

It is not just in the blooming of foreign flower fields that we witness the hospitality of flowers. We marvel at the centerpieces of the tables at a wedding feast or restaurant and how they beckon us to linger and enjoy. Artisans have used images of flowers for millennia to adorn woodwork, metalwork, fabric, and paintings, and serve as a perpetual source of welcome in countless rooms. Flowers come to greet us in everyday things and enhance so much of ordinary life. They serve as a beautiful backdrop for all

that happens in life, whether at home or abroad. And, though we rest from our work in the garden, the beauty of God's abundance is ever-present to us in our respite.

———————

"When we see a beautiful object, a beautiful garden or
a beautiful flower, let us think that there we behold
a ray of the infinite beauty of God,
who has given existence to that object."

—SAINT ALPHONSUS LIGUORI

———————

Design

In the height of summertime, the pairing of focal blooms with vines makes a beautiful combination. The arrangements are similar, though different, to the drooping bulbs of spring and resemble an English garden distilled into a vase. As dahlias seem to be the stand-out flower of the month, it seems only fitting to permit their basking in the limelight with a fine dainty structure provided by honeysuckle vines. However, any large-headed focal flower will do in creating the winding vines and the blooms of the loose garden design.

The Resurgence of the Dutch Masters

The Netherlands' expansive economic and political influence and cultural achievements during the seventeenth century have historically become known as the Dutch Golden Age. Successful, far-reaching trade routes brought about immigration and prosperity for the tiny nation. Exotic flora and foodstuffs made their way by ship onto the shores of the North Sea from across the globe. This time of affluence facilitated an era of innumerable accomplishments, most notably within the arts field. The burgeoning merchant class commissioned the work of magnificent artists such as Rembrandt van Rijn, Peter Brueghel the Elder, and Ambrosius Bosschaert to adorn the walls of their fashionable homes.

Dutch Masters, affectionately known as the Old Masters, perfectly captured the beauty of the ordinary. Kitchen and laundry scenes, though mundane, were elevated as a scene to take in and ponder when put to canvas or wood. The rendering of the average aspects of life in works of art highlights the subtle beauty of everyday life.

Similarly, the Old Masters' renderings of florals are breathtaking. For many, these are the still-life renderings that first come to mind when discussing the paintings of the Dutch Golden Era. Drooping, dramatic tulips graze the table, filled with endless varieties of roses and vines bursting forth from the middle, contrasted by towering Crown Imperial Fritillaria. Flowers grown in faraway places were shipped across the vast oceans and rendered in oil to live for eternity. Often appearing in these paintings were non-floral items that developed a profound story of *memento mori*, offering a sobering reminder that all is transient. These paintings were difficult to produce at the time and arranged by the strokes

of paintbrushes, as they included flora that spanned seasons and many climates from across the globe. The arrangements' style is perfectly reminiscent of the gardens from which the flowers came: simultaneously wild and contained and, above all, unbelievably romantic.

The artistry of these masterpieces is so timeless that they have made a resurgence and are trendsetting still several hundred years later, knocking aside the spheric and symmetrical arrangements made prominent by the Victorian era. Stumbling upon the work of the Dutch Masters was highly formative for me as a floral apprentice. I am grateful for the increased interest in the masterpieces of a bygone era that both prized and perfectly captured the wonder of the flower.

September

September brings a hurriedness filled with the winds of change. Everyone behaves like busy bees in intense preparation as both man and beast hustle and bustle. It is a time of movement as birds begin to migrate south in preparation for the colder days ahead. Families adjust to their new flight patterns as school and activities get underway. Over the month, a cool autumn breeze replaces the humid summer air. Spider lilies appear out of nowhere with their long stamens. A sea of goldenrod flowers roll in waves as far as the eye can see, their rich golden hue rivaled only by the sun of the late summer sky. Soft and luxurious lamb's ear anchors the garden through the year but reaches its fullest potential as summer's flowers begin to fade. Their blue-green coloring uniquely softens a bright color palette. Coneflower is a great focal of the garden and vase as their prickly, sturdy visages are fitting during this time of year. Autumn-blooming azaleas showcase their showy flowers before resting during the colder seasons. Days are growing shorter—all that was green fades to copper and brown by month's end as flowers dry on the stem.

Like March and June, September is a transitional month. One season gives way to another. The months that overlap seasons have formed a special place in my heart. They are enigmatic and inevitably wild, a time of unpredictable weather. They are an *entr'acte* of sorts, but a unique act unto themselves. September is set apart in its manner of bridging summer to fall. We both put to rest and start anew within the same month. Children return to school, and new beginnings abound. Yet, a great deal of outdoor work ends once the harvest is complete.

"Today it still is summer
tomorrow will be fall.
I see the purple asters,
I hear the autumn's call."

—NONA KEEN DUFFY

In the eastern half of the United States, the threats of hurricanes loom during September when the ocean temperature reaches its warmest. It is always fascinating but frightening to witness nature seemingly at war with itself as a mighty storm threatens anything in its path. Before late summer of 2021, I had never experienced the strength of a hurricane as it transitions

from water onto land, but all that changed as Hurricane Ida made her way inland from the Gulf of Mexico. As darkness began to fall, we piled into our old off-road vehicle to drive to the highest part of the property to watch Hurricane Ida's outer bands roll in, preceding the storm, with fast-moving clouds bringing increasing winds and sprinkles of rain. Unsure of what to expect during my first southern hurricane, I could only be in awe of the beauty and immensity of the storm in the distance. Hours later, the wonder turned to concern as the howling winds ripped through, slapping an unsecured shutter open and shut with abandon while simultaneously testing the pliable limits of trees and plants. In natural disasters, we witness the strength and durability of nature. Trees and plants bend in the wind but often withstand the test.

———————

"In all places, then, and in all seasons,
flowers expand their light and soul-like wings,
teaching us, by most persuasive reasons,
how akin they are to human things."

—HENRY WADSWORTH LONGFELLOW

———————

It was after the experience of Hurricane Ida that I learned of the astonishing story of the Peggy Martin rose. Years earlier, Katrina had ravaged Louisiana and Mississippi with abandon, destroying all in its path. The coastal region was under twenty feet of salt water, killing all vegetation and taking human life. Despite being in the hurricane's indiscriminate path, one rose survived being submerged for two weeks. The rose had no name at the time, as it was a propagation from an unknown rosebush species. It later bore the name of Peggy Martin, for the house's gardener where it survived. Propagations of the rose began to be sold, raising money for the restoration efforts

of destroyed southern gardens. Years later, the rose is still beloved, as friends generously share clippings. One glance at the beautiful rambling rose bears witness to the resiliency and perseverance of the people and the planet.

"The flower that blooms in adversity
is the rarest and most beautiful of all."
—CHINESE PROVERB

In the storms of life, we can look to the garden and see all it has endured: rain, wind, drought, and ice, elements outside of their control, to be reminded that we can thrive in adversity. When all seems lost, we must remember that nothing is impossible for God, who even spares a rose as a visible reminder of His faithfulness during trials. The cross reminds us of the redemptive nature

of suffering. We continue to live out this reality today. God uses our afflictions brought about by the world to help others. Through our own experience of suffering, we attain genuine empathy and create in us the desire to limit and assuage the grief of others. What we undergo galvanizes us so that we, like the Peggy Martin rose, can bless others in their hardship.

As the heat of summer collapses into the crisper days of autumn, we are also altered by these winds of change. Our daily habits have shifted and migrated, like birds in flight, away from the tiring garden. The sun's warm gaze retreats during the months of autumn, and so do we, back into the comforting "nest" of our homes.

Design

Of all the flowering shrubs, hydrangeas might be the most beautiful. There is a variety of hydrangeas to suit any taste. Not only do they vary in color and shape but within each there is also a beautiful progression of color as it matures. They stand alone beautifully in a vase, with or without foliage, and are equally stunning in an arrangement with other types of flowers. Drying beautifully, they also maintain a marvelous display for a long time. Sedum and yarrow are two wonderful filler flowers that come to the fullness of blooming in September. Many other summer blooms remain and put on a fantastic show in the garden. When arranging hydrangea with other flowers, it is best to keep the head of the hydrangea low in the arrangement, almost against the rim of the vase, creating a dynamic of layers that doesn't overshadow the rest of the design.

Handheld Still Life Devotional: Book of Hours

When we think about the Middle Ages, our minds fill with images of castles and small villages set against a pastoral way of life, with large monasteries in the distance housing pious monks. During most of the medieval period, the majority of the population were members of the lowest class within feudal society. The rise of trade during the latter half of the Middle Ages enabled a new merchant class.

Life in the medieval period meant close connectivity to the land, especially for the peasants or villeins. Working on the land resulted in a deep sensitivity to the cyclic part of nature. The rhythmic element of the seasons meant that work differed significantly from month to month. Time spent resting in the winter months differed from the toils of spring, summer, and fall. Time was fluid between work and prayer within the monastery walls and the life of a layperson of every social class. Painters have captured field workers pausing for prayer at the Angelus bell. The Psalters, or Books of the Hours, are helpful prayer books modeled after the Divine Office recited at certain times of day in monasteries. These were a treasured possession of the lay faithful of nobility. But, with the development of the merchant class, more books were created as the demand significantly increased.

The ability to own handheld and bound still-life artworks to use as a devotional tool for the laity was one of the most beautiful gifts of the Middle Ages. The illustrations found within the Book of Hours often contained arresting paintings of feast days or scenes from the life of Christ. The Labors of the Months within these devotionals reflected the seasons' rhythm and work completed throughout the year. These bound works of art aided the faithful

as a devotional tool to facilitate a more profound prayer time that mimicked monastic life. Labors of the Months are in the most beautiful and sacred structures: Chartres Cathedral, Notre Dame Cathedral, Canterbury Cathedral, and many more.

The reader quickly identified each month from the activity illuminated on the page. Books were customized according to the region. However, the same Labors of the Months took place whether in Northern or Southern Europe. There were differences in the crops cultivated in the region according to the people for whom artists created the Book of Hours. A common Book of the Hours would showcase the following:

- January depicted scenes of feasting and New Year's gift exchanges.

- February depicted scenes of sitting by the fire, gathering firewood, and digging or pruning.

- March depicted the preparation of the soil by plowing and the pruning of vines.

- April depicted the blossoming of trees, picking of flowers, and planting in fields.

- May depicted scenes of courting, enjoying nature, and hawking.

- June depicted the toil of hay harvesting in the fields.

- July depicted the toil of wheat harvesting and sheep being shorn.

- August depicted the threshing of wheat.

- September depicted the grape harvesting from the vines pruned in March.

- October depicted ploughing and sowing of grain and wine making.

- November depicted acorns being fed to the pigs to fatten them for harvest.

- December depicted hog butchering and hunting for boar for January feasting.

The instant recognition of each month's labor speaks to the predictability of the seasons. The work in the land by peasants marks time. The predictable progression throughout the year is a great comfort. These beautiful manuscripts illustrate the holiness of everyday work as it coincides with prayer.

AUTUMN

When the rush of harvest follows summer's toil into the pile of days gone by, our focus turns toward comfort. Autumn air smells of the warm spices, and the once green leaves put on fiery displays. So much seems to change in an instant as the days begin to shorten significantly. The sun hangs lower in the sky as its angled golden rays beam through tree branches. When daylight saving time ends, darkness swallows the day. Efforts for coziness abound in the season's rituals as the presence of the sun diminishes. We find solace by the fireplace where wood is aflame, made possible by an enduring gift from the outdoors, comforting us in our rest. Life unfolds within the home, beside the newly awoken fireplace; smoke billows from the chimney and delights noses up and down the block.

The garden enters a mode of preservation and energy conservation for survival during the coming months. As the warmth wanes, threats of frost increase with each passing day. The gardener closes the work of the garden with the hopeful planting of those spring bulbs that produce the first joys upon winter's retreat.

Once more, we gather outdoors with friends and family around grand bonfires. Nature's backdrop has changed from the year's first lush and verdant gatherings in the garden to crisp and amber. We cook our food on long sticks grazing the flames that warm us. Gazing attentively at the blaze, we are recollected in a unique way.

Autumn provides the time to reflect upon the joys and gifts of spring and summer while preparing for winter. We ponder the successes and failures of the year retrospectively, just as we do during the "autumn of our lives."

"No spring nor summer beauty hath such grace
as I have seen in one autumnal face."

–JOHN DONNE

As pumpkins and gourds fill the home, cornstalks adorn the outdoor posts in a rejoiceful manner for the bountiful harvest. Laughing children jump into piles of raked leaves. Remaining leaves crunch underfoot. Large fluffy mums billow from the terracotta pots edging the walkway to the front door. It is an enchanting time of year within which we whisper farewell to the flowery landscape. Despite the succession of goodbyes, there are still flowers in shades of copper and plum, with an excess of texture, ready to make an appearance in the home.

The Tender Tension
between Gardener and Florist

There is a constant tension between gardeners and florists. A florist desires to cut each blooming stem into a vase, while the gardener wishes to treasure the bloom as it grows. The more profoundly involved one becomes in either pursuit, the more torn the individual. Watching the hopeful flower buds form on a rose to eventually blow wide open within the context of a garden landscape, I am conflicted. They are so breathtaking to witness as they delicately open that I do not want to disturb them. But then I imagine it spilling over the lip of my favorite patinaed brass urn, and I cannot wait to remove every stem to enjoy its beauty and fragrance from within my home. There is a reward for maintaining a balance between the two competing desires, and an immense benefit in allowing flowers to bloom and remain on the plant, eventually turning to seed to be collected the following year. Simultaneously, the beauty of flowers enriches our homes through their presence.

The existence of a cutting garden is extremely helpful in resolving the struggle. The sole purpose of such a garden is the cutting of all the flowers to bring indoors. One can cut with abandon and not worry about diminishing the garden's look. But if planting a separate cutting garden is not possible due to space restrictions, I have found that the best way to ease the fear of over-harvesting from the garden is by keeping half of the flowers on the plants and harvesting half to enjoy inside. Another great option is to tuck flower seeds among the rows of a vegetable garden to cut and enjoy.

Experimenting by planting annual flower seeds is a great way to begin a cutting garden. They are a low investment purchase and tend to be great flowers to work with, like zinnia, larkspur, sunflower, or calendula. There are also perennial flowers that are easy to grow and great to cut, like coneflower, phlox, or yarrow. Harvesting some seeds by letting a few stems remain on the plant until thoroughly dried is a wonderfully inexpensive way to continue and grow a cutting garden for years to come.

October

Oh, October, how easy you are to love, the month when we view the world through pumpkin-spiced glasses! It is clear why Anne of Green Gables could not contain her joy as she exclaimed that she was so glad to "live in a world where there are Octobers." As the air develops its striking autumnal scent and crispness, we dress in oversized scarves and flannel, surrounded by blossoming mums. We decorate with pumpkins and sip warm beverages, and fireside chats and the glow of lamp light illuminate our nights. The world turns into shades of warm comfort. The leaves, as they age, put on a magnificent and fiery display before dropping to nourish the soil.

Unique color is injected into the landscape from blooming asters. Luscious butterfly bush in rich colors attract endless butterflies and hummingbirds. Monkshood cowl-like petals seem to prayerfully gaze upon the earth. Japanese anemones are an ideal airy flower. Their charming personality enhances shade gardens and autumn flower arrangements. Though the diversity of flowers available dwindle in this season, those that are present put on a tremendous display.

As the landscape turns green to brown, all goes to seed, dries, and appears dead. But this is when we secure the future of the garden. As the wind blows, it takes tiny seeds through the air to spread (or be collected by hand to save and plant). October is a forward-gazing time, not in a state of anxious and inactive waiting like winter, but instead one of preparation. We plant bulbs and collect seeds from dried flowers, all in careful readiness for the future.

We cultivate flowers like a home: slowly, lovingly, intentionally. Tending a garden also helps to create certain habits of being within ourselves. Though to garden is to toil and far from glamorous, the fruit this work bears is enduring. As the days collect into weeks and months, it is easier to see the year's progression. Cooperation with God to do our work in the garden induces patience from an early age. Little children plant seeds in small cups and learn to patiently wait before finally witnessing signs of growth. It is easy to see the exponential growth within the garden over time, leading to greater understanding, patience, and self-control.

"So many little flowers
Drop their tiny heads
But newer buds come to bloom
In their place instead. I miss the little flowers
That have gone away.
But the newly budding blossoms
Are equally gay."

—LANGSTON HUGHES

As we gaze into a flower, often people in our lives are called to mind; a sentiment well captured in the lyrics of "The Very Thought of You" written by Ray Noble, sung famously by Nat King Cole in which he intones, "I see your face in every flower." These words came to my mind one day when a postcard arrived in the mail from my former neighbor, Katherine, painted with the most exquisite roses. She wrote that these roses were reminiscent of the garden I planted at my old house, which now sits 1,200 miles away. This

little card was a gift in so many ways. I had been missing the flowers of that established garden as I worked to build new gardens from scratch. I longed to reap the tremendous benefits from years of loving toil. As I read the post-card, a thought humbled me that, though we garden for ourselves and those around us, cultivating a garden often brings beauty into the lives of those we may never meet. So often we do not witness the actualization of our arduous work, much like Moses preparing for land he never entered. Planting a garden establishes an inheritance, whether for the next owner of the house or the next generation.

> "The care of the earth is our most ancient and most worthy,
> and after all our most pleasing responsibility.
> To cherish what remains of it and to
> foster its renewal is our only hope."
>
> —WENDELL BERRY

Tending to a garden makes it possible for flowers to exist for the next generation. Similarly, we seek to cultivate and instill a faith culture to pass on to our descendants. It is in this way that growing flowers are akin to raising children, as we need to nurture, tend to, and protect them. This process requires an immense amount of patience. But after planting seeds, we pray for a strong establishment of roots, supported by the proper nutrients, to weather any storm and bear new fruit for generations to come. It is our life's work to cultivate within those entrusted to us a devotion for the good, true, and beautiful rooted in memory and love that carries through the generations.

A lovely woman, Debra Devereaux, whose family came from Italy, tells a story of the gardens of her grandparents. Deep within her memory is the narrow sidewalk that wove between her grandparents' flower and food gardens.

Beauty and function collided with love in these green spaces outside their Spanish villa. Butterflies and ladybugs captured the awe of the grandchildren. They happily meandered the pathway that teemed with orange, tangerine, and lemon trees toward the large trellis containing the objects of their desire: the deepest, richest, most flavorful concord grapes. Her Nonni and Nonno spent every waking moment in their gardens and beckoned the company of others there. As children, they grew up within the poorer class in Sicily and learned the importance of growing their food to survive. In their life in Southern California, however, it became a major source of hospitality; a guest never left without a bounty of fresh fruit and vegetables lovingly grown. But to Debra, this garden was a grand inheritance. It was a backdrop to a rich life that she seeks to preserve and pass on to her grandchildren. She jokes with her sisters—somewhat winsomely—that she aims to "get back to Nonni's garden" with each planting addition to her garden. Debra's story of her replication of her grandparents' beautiful garden is easily relatable to our own stories as we seek to recreate the gifts of our childhood while we raise the next generations of our family.

"Every leaf speaks bliss to me,
fluttering from the autumn tree."

—EMILY BRONTE

We are wise to spend our consolation in slow, intentional preparation for desolation—the spiritual practice of creating stores of grace aids in those times of trial. In like manner, we should use the abundance of the harvest. Drying flowers is a beautiful act in anticipation of the leaner times of winter. They make a fantastic, everlasting display.

Additionally, flower heads left on the plant to dry are helpful for seed collection. One flower produces an overabundance of seeds, and a new possibility of beauty comes from each tiny seed. As we collect small little seeds, we hold the flowers of tomorrow.

When collecting seeds at the season's end, we witness God's provision that sustains us from generation to generation. That which bears good fruit will be an endless source of beauty for years. Flowers build upon flowers into continuity and perpetuity within which we find continual enjoyment. The flowers of yesterday are connected to the ones of tomorrow by way of seeds. In my parents' garden grows a boxwood raised from clippings from my great-grandmother's farm. Family legend has it that these great bushes sprouted from cuttings from Colonial Williamsburg. These threads of continuity transcend space and time, bonding mankind. As we cultivate gardens, we establish something that extends beyond our fingertips and affects the lives of others. This is the beautiful work of our maker, the Creator of the universe, that we are so blessed to take part in.

Design

As spring and summer flower arrangements evoke a feeling of vitality, autumnal arrangements impart a feeling of comfort. The flowers and branches of earthy, rich tones and decadent textures are never-ending. It is another beautiful time to decorate with branches, like spring, but this time showcasing deep romantic hues in the leaves. The last round of zinnias bloom in the garden, intermixing with steadily opening buds of chrysanthemums. I love the backdrop of bunches of flowers hanging to dry throughout the house. Bushels of wheat, cornstalks, and tufts of grasses blend the outdoor landscape with the warmth of home. Japanese lanterns and bittersweets are uniquely autumnal touches of nature. Of course, there is great joy in decorating with pumpkins and gourds. Creativity abounds as textures and earth-tone hues are at our fingertips. I love to refresh the typical colors of gold, orange, and red with pops of pastels and dusty shades in blues, pinks, and greens.

How to Make a Boutonniere

Possessing the knowledge of how to make a boutonniere—these "little bouquets"—is surprisingly helpful. If you can make a boutonniere, you can make a flower crown (a series of boutonnieres taped along a wire), a bouquet, and much more.

A boutonniere is easy to construct. First, you must gather your items. These include a small focal bloom—for example, one head of a small spray rose, a tiny bit of greenery, and one or two bits of texture (berries, small celosia growth, a piece of ornamental grass, or so many other options). Once you have what you need, follow these directions:

- Like constructing a bouquet, begin with your focal bloom and place one or two pieces of the texture to "cup" the focal flower.

  Pro tip: If using a spray rose, reinforce it using a small gauge wire, poking it through the rounded portion where the stem meets the petals, pushing about one inch of wire through and bending it down to follow the stem and securing it with tape.

- Tape the stems together using floral tape, making sure you pull with a bit of tension to "activate" the stickiness. Only a few wraps of tape will be needed to secure.

  Pro tip: If using a spray rose, make it less prone to breaking by piercing floral wire through the base of the head of the flower, known as the "hip," and using floral tape to tape the wire into place.

- Add a small leaf to create structure in the back.

  Optional: finish with a tiny piece of greenery placed on the front side.

- Wrap the stems several times with floral tape to secure. Cover the tape by wrapping a thin piece of ribbon around the stems. Tuck two straight pins to secure on clothing later. Keep the boutonniere in the refrigerator until ready to use. It can be made two to three days before the event.

Pro tip: When securing the boutonniere, placing one pin up and one pin down will keep it secure on the clothing and prevent it from the dreaded sideways tilt.

November

The roses of November burst out in one last blooming rebellion against the sleeping landscape before retreating into rose hips. We are surprised at the realization that there are as many varieties of ornamental grasses as there are flowers: tall and billowy, petite and rabbit-tailed, deep purple and wispy, and many more. Chrysanthemums of all shapes and sizes ranging from spider-like to pillow-like are the main show of the month. Black-eyed Susans end their long, vibrant season as hardy sedum and Russian sage implant contrasting pastel hues.

Foggy mornings envelop the world at sunrise, blending the earth and sky into a poetic ambiance of a month that combines remembrance and thanksgiving. We find comfort in the reality that though the seasons change, God is constant and unchanging, bringing a grounded sense to our days with the conclusion of the year. Nature reveals the days gone by, highlighting that the months passed in the year are far greater in number than those remaining. Autumn is reflected through the lens of the idiom "the autumn of our lives," speaking to a specific season of life. Despite this, it is an immense season of hope: in planting bulbs, letting flowers go to seed, and in the season's rich colors. Despite the reminder that the "bloom falls from the rose," it is also the time of a bountiful harvest. Wherein we reap the benefits of the fruits of the summer and collect seeds so that beauty may live.

In the United States, it is the month of Thanksgiving celebrations, a day of the gathering of loved ones. The booming laughter and bumping of elbows from boarding house reaches fills the space of the celebration that brings us to the same table from near and far. We spend time in gratitude for those sitting around the table and those whose seats have become empty over the years. This month, we return to the *memento mori* we encountered in the winter. The mortality of the landscape is ever before us. As the life of a flower ends in beautiful decay, it returns to the soil, its source of life.

"It was November—the month of crimson sunsets,
parting birds, deep, sad hymns of the sea,
passionate wind-songs in the pines."

–LUCY MAUD MONTGOMERY

The flower's life cycle points to the reality that we, along with the lilies of the field, will be resigned to withering and returning to the soil. All the while, we are reminded of the wonder to behold in each stage. Nature works in both cyclic and linear patterns. Seasons come and go perpetually, yet the individual's life is linear, a reality that consoles. As we progress in years, we find hope and comfort that the world goes on with its usual ebb and flow, with a visual thread of continuity as springtime always returns. Meditating upon the landscape as it returns to the soil is a powerful witness. As we gaze, we remember that the process of aging is a gift, and though beauty has changed from the "fresh" days, it still exists. We also recognize that from death comes life anew. The annual reminder of our mortality is

an invaluable kindling that reignites the motivation to make the best use of our time. Through complacency and comfort, we fall prey to sloth. As we witness the death of the landscape, we recall that we cannot reclaim the days passed. There is immense importance in the seeds that we plant; in a sense, they bind us to a future of hope. To wit, we reclaim our senses and become rooted in the present.

"Wild is the music of autumnal winds
amongst the faded woods."

—WILLIAM WORDSWORTH

All Saints and All Souls Days are significant feast days of commemoration of the beloved dead. We pray that those we love may ultimately bask in the beatific vision, while invoking the aid of those already in heaven. These days epitomize what we pray in the Nicene Creed as we look forward to "the resurrection of the dead and the life of the world to come." In these feasts, we

find an additional focus, aside from Mass, on the connection between heaven and earth, serving as a humbling reminder of the expansion of our hearts and homes between two worlds. I have many childhood memories of adorning the graves of our departed family members. My mother would forage greens and arrange several sprays to place at their graves, the homes of their eternal rest. An entire day would be spent visiting the graves of our loved ones, often braving the weather while lighting candles and recounting memories. These acts are essential to remembering the dead and keeping their memories alive and, we pray, experiencing the joy of reunification.

"The soil is the great connector of lives,
the source and destination of all.
It is the healer and restorer and resurrector,
by which disease passes into health,
age into youth, death into life."

—WENDELL BERRY

The grave is an extension of the home, as it is where our loved ones are. When they leave us, our places expand to include the ground within which they are buried. Decorating these spaces communicates the same love and affection we shared in life. This humble token of gratitude visualizes what G. K. Chesterton wrote about the importance of the "democracy of the dead" to whom we owe a great deal and with whom we remain connected. Those who came before us laid a foundation through millennia that aids us in this most sacred journey home to the Father. Knowledge built upon knowledge, as beauty instructed beauty. The dead have a tremendous legacy that demands acknowledgment and love. As Roger

Scruton says, "Those who have lost respect for their dead have ceased to be trustees of their inheritance." As we see in the life of faith, God transcends time and place wherein He bridges heaven and earth, something most evident in November as the Church winds down the last weeks of the liturgical calendar.

"So go the flowers place to place
The sweetest friends of the human race;
Then finally the last place of all
Upon men's graves they gladly fall,
And lie there dreaming with their friends
Flowers with flowers, as the long day ends."

—EDWIN CURRAN

Flowers serve as a tangible connection to our departed loved ones. We witness how flowers enhance our humanity. They console us in grief, triumph with us in joy, and brighten everyday moments in life. They are a reminder that despite our circumstances, beauty remains and consoles. They have a constancy; when all else comes and goes, beauty and God endure, which is why flowers bring such consolation in their permanency, even in dormancy. They are a reminder that, though we all face certain death, abundant life lies beyond in renewed hope. We owe a debt of gratitude to past and future generations for being intentional custodians of beauty in the world.

Design

November is a beautiful opportunity to add engaging, conversation-starting elements to arrangements. The garden contains a treasure trove of attractive seed pods and branches that will make a wonderfully unique flower arrangement. Dried pods, tree branches, grasses, and produce are some excellent ways to create exciting textures and layers. The use of food in a design is also a fun play on the traditional American Thanksgiving cornucopia. I love using lettuces, artichokes, kumquats, lemons or oranges, and beets, to name a few. Chrysanthemums in all sizes and shades are available in abundance. Roses are also gathered and adored for their one final bloom of the year.

December

Tension is ever-present as the calendar turns to December and autumn draws to a close to welcome the restful duration of winter. Nature's composition changes once more. Regular frosts return to the sleeping garden as nature slips gently back into winter at the month's end. All red-berried shrubs—nandina, holly, and Christmas berry—are aglow. Camellia buds burst open to greet the year's end. The foliage of paperwhites emerge from the soil in anticipation of the New Year. The bright colors of winterberry exist as a stark beauty in great contrast to the naked landscape. The darkened berries of crepe myrtle create a wondrous texture to the garden. Hellebores delicately tucked against the cold earth reawaken. Evergreens stand out as the only source of emerald color in the landscape.

We pare down in preparation to welcome the source of all life: the Word made flesh. It is a stripped-down month as trees lay bare, yet one of plenty as December is home to the start of the heavily ornamental Christmas season. In the seemingly barren weeks of Advent, hymns of the expectant awaiting of the Messiah rise from the pews. Children construct paper chains and collect pieces of straw for nativity scenes with empty mangers to visualize the virtuous deeds completed throughout the four weeks of Advent.

December tests our resolve to be comfortable in the wait. This time enables the blossoming of the lessons taught throughout the year, specifically those of having contentment along life's journey. Autumn, as well as winter, exists in a period between the former in nature and the forthcoming. As there is a sense of limbo, what we need most is to find rest in the *not yet*. Saint Teresa of Calcutta reminds us to "be happy in the moment, that's enough. Each moment is all we need, not more." We find special gratitude in having peace in the present.

————————

"This Flow'r, whose fragrance tender
With sweetness fills the air,
Dispels with glorious splendor
The darkness everywhere.
True man, yet very God,
From sin and death He saves us,
And lightens every load."

−FRIEDRICH LAYRITZ, *LO HOW A ROSE E'ER BLOOMING*

————————

With the commencement of Advent, the Church's calendar begins again. All things end to make room for new beginnings in nature and within our hearts. Advent is a sacred season of waiting and watching for Christ's coming. Yet, the secular world seeks to accelerate through the anticipatory wait. A temptation exists to join the world in the forgoing of this prayerful time and proceed immediately to the fun of Christmas. Gleaning from the intentionality of the seasons, we see it applies to so much in life.

Advent is an extraordinary time because of its prayerful waiting. Our attentiveness is at a height, ever more sensitive to Christ's coming because of the stillness found in the wait. We have learned throughout the year that we

often have the most interior growth in these barren times. Years ago, during the Collect of Sunday Mass in Advent, we prayed, "grant your faithful . . . Almighty God, the resolve to run forth to meet Your Christ with righteous deeds at His coming." Our Lord comes to us at Christmas in the quietest of ways, hidden within the still of the night. In such a calm that I can say confidently, after years of inattentive Advents, I missed His coming.

It is often in these unyielding times that we have the most growth. In the past, I have rushed into the "most wonderful time of the year," but Christmas after observing the pregnant pause of Advent is much richer. There is no overdosing on Christmas cheer, and no hangover either.

A Christmas celebration after the pregnant pause of Advent is much more prosperous due to the filling of a longing that only Christ can satiate. But first we must fast to uncouple ourselves from our distractive attachments that otherwise preoccupy the space for the good, the true, and the beautiful. As we put aside the world's distractions—namely, the pre-Christmas rush—in preparation for Christ's birth, we prayerfully create a space for God. Distractions tether us to the ground when we should be rushing toward the Lord upon His coming, like the shepherds and Magi. It is an unrivaled gift to viscerally feel the waiting of figures like Simeon and Anna, whose joy becomes palpable upon the news of the Messiah's birth.

"There is no peace that cannot be found in the present moment."

—TASHA TUDOR

Saint Bernard of Clairvaux said that it is in silence that we can prepare. It is difficult to feel as if we are in preparation when our homes brim with the signs that the feast is already here. We can process, learn, and grow from life's occurrences in the quiet. A harried, distracted life provides little calm for this. The two millennia wisdom of the Church is evident during Advent, in which the stillness of the liturgical season rivals the world's frantic posture. She knows we need a quiet time of fasting and preparing for the greatest gift the world has ever received. She knows that Ordinary Time alone does not provide adequate preparation. We must sing certain hymns, recite specific prayers, and observe certain colors, all for a particular purpose, as physical reminders that help cultivate slowness and stillness within.

My hectic Advents of the past brimmed with endless lists of Christmas activities that resulted in a sense of relief once Christmas had ended. I missed God's whisper in the noise. Instead of a watchful wait, all the "doing" during the Advent season distracted me from a quiet, peaceful readiness to run toward Him when He beckons. Without shiny distractions, we can maintain an attentive gaze, look East, and witness the Lord's coming.

An excellent relationship exists between beauty and slowness of pace. Slowing permits a better posture to encounter beauty while the encounter relaxes us further. Contemplation of beauty places us into what Jean-Pierre de Caussade calls the "Sacrament of the Present Moment," within which we attain an attentive posture. We are particular and intuitive in a state of attentiveness, with a deep focus and disregard for erroneous noise and distraction. Allowing ourselves to be present is the best weapon in our fight against the tyranny of the urgent fueled by utilitarianism, pulling in all different paths that lead to nowhere.

In being present, we push aside all that is an obstacle, making a pathway available for the Great Pursuer. We begin to see God all around, present in every moment and within the hearts of those around us. Through our stillness, we can hear that small, quiet voice within. Here in this contemplation, we find God. As we recollect ourselves and become aware of the presence of the Lord in the day-to-day, we find refuge and solace and become better prepared for His coming.

There is seamlessness in seasonal living and bringing nature into our homes in December. It is a time in which the focus is on fragrant evergreens, which stand out against the stripped-down landscape. Advent wreaths adorn our spaces, and we light candles, marking the countdown to the coming of the Savior. Jesse trees keep the days of Advent as we prepare for Christ's birth by the daily meditation upon each chapter of salvation history. As purple gives way to the bright shades of red and green, the joy of Christ's birth manifests. Like little Creches, our hearts, minds, and homes have been primed in the wait to receive Him. We adorn large fragrant trees with personal trinkets and tokens. These practices, like the bounty found in nature, transcend time and place, connecting the faithful through the generations through tradition.

"What day is it?"
"It's today," squeaked Piglet.
"My favorite day," said Pooh.

Easing back into the quiet of winter provides a renewed opportunity for rest that carries us through the New Year. The beautiful break in fasting with Christmas helps us persist through winter's dark days. The persistence of the darkness over the day is a sobering reminder that, at times, the world is dark. It always has been and always will be. But this same world contains an endless wealth of beauty. It always has and will continue to. We can only control the darkness and beauty that resides within our souls. Beauty is light, pointing us to Him and shining and persisting in the darkness. We can create beauty with our hands, multiply it within ourselves, and share it to change the world. With the birth of the world's light, we recall that God makes all things new and our perspective, and homes, change. As the year's pilgrimage concludes,

our resolve for heaven is bolstered. Though we may get lost in a particular season, the cycles of the months root and ground us. It is my hope that through barren and plenty we observe our place on the map—"you are here"—and find joy.

Design

Though flowers are sparse, there are lovely things to cut and arrange into a container. Through the closing of autumn, I have loved working with preserved and dried flowers. Wreaths and mantles are fitting places to adorn with dried stems. There is an understated elegance in a vase of freshly cut evergreen branches. Layering various types of foliage makes a beautifully dramatic statement in a room. Juniper berries, privet berries, and wide varieties of red berries make for a great texture against an arrangement of foliage. Of course, the Advent Wreath is the centerpiece of the month, with its candles reminding us that the Light will break through the darkness. I love making a simple evergreen wreath to hang on the front door throughout December to embellish at Christmas. Slicing and drying oranges are a fragrant and appealing way of adorning the home. But no matter what we do, by month's end, all is overshadowed by the radiant splendor of the Christmas tree and potted Poinsettias!

Christmas

As Advent makes its way to a close, the air is teeming with anticipation. Touches of purple and rose are replaced by festive red and green as old boxes come out of the attic filled with decorations collected over the years. During the four weeks of Advent, the season of hope and joy is long-awaited. Christmas is the height of bringing nature inside the home.

The Church has consistently celebrated Christ's birth since the fourth century. During those years, Christmas decorations have changed, but tiny threads of continuity have been maintained over time, something that has been made most evident in the Church. Some of these ancient traditions exist in the modern home. One is decorating the house with freshly cut greens in the form of garlands, dried oranges, wreaths, swags, and Christmas trees. Memory and smell are firmly linked, and for many, the smell of freshly cut evergreen is synonymous with Christmas. The Christmas tree is the main feature of yuletide home decor, but the other festive touches of evergreens also communicate the season's celebration of enduring joy by way of their symbolic permanence of green.

A beloved pastime of mine is foraging nature's bounty to bring the beauty inside my home—a hobby most obvious at Christmastime. Encountering God in creation and discovering evidence of that experience within your home is a poetic way to decorate at Christmastime. It's equally remarkable to make use of this bounty to prepare our homes for the coming of Christ. It is invigorating to stroll outside to hunt for blooms and greens, and I love the frugality. Items harvested from the wild also tend to have more personality than can be found in a store and are more enjoyable to use in designs.

Lastly, the greens will have greater longevity being freshly cut rather than purchased from a store.

Foraging for evergreen cuttings is happily straightforward. In December, we can cut green things and use them to deck the halls. While pine is the most used evergreen for Christmas garlands, other options abound. Many forms of greenery are festive. Where you call home plays a significant role in the types of greens available. Using what is readily available in your region helps to make your design special. If you don't have access to a place where you can snip greens, head to a Christmas tree farm or lot—they often have discarded trimmings that are given away or sold at a steep discount.

The way we deck our halls is personal. No two homes or memories are the same. Much is born from tradition unique to each family, reflecting intimately and intentionally the personal way God comes to us. For centuries, evergreens have been brought into the home to decorate for Christmas. The use of evergreens as decoration at this time of year is symbolic of everlasting life found in Christ as the leaves of these trees do not dry and fall from the branch. Pine and fir clippings are most common and readily available in many populated regions. But many great options can also be used: boxwood, pittosporum, magnolia, cedar, cypress, et cetera. Shrubs with red berries give a wonderfully merry touch.

The magic of Christmas makes it easy to become enamored with the tangible things of the season. We must remember as we decorate that we are preparing our homes to receive the One who was once intangible made flesh: the Word Incarnate. We deck the halls to showcase that which stands out from the rest this time. We marvel at the Eucharistic poetry of the God-man born and placed

into a manger, which just so happens to be a French infinitive form of the verb meaning "to eat." We bridge the old year with the new as we bring the everlasting gifts of creation into our homes to celebrate the coming of the One who redeemed the world.

Hail and blessed be the hour and moment in which the Son of God was born of the purest Virgin Mary in Bethlehem, in the piercing cold night.

The World Is a Garden

The garden is an extension of our homes, and our homes an extension of the garden. Within the greenhouse-like nature of a home, life is nurtured. Delicate saplings grow under protection to prepare for the trials of the outside elements. An ill-timed introduction is detrimental to a fragile life. It is at home that we cultivate the environment in such a way as to facilitate the best growth for life within.

The world can still be a garden, whether the home is an urban apartment, an expansive rural estate, or something in between. Whether this "bit of earth" is in your possession or in the care of those maintaining a botanical garden, the encounter with green spaces is necessary. In the garden's beauty, we rest in awe and wonder of God's creation and witness His power and love, He who formed the waters and land for our benefit. That which changes us in our encounter with the great expanses, we seek to bring into our homes to enjoy in everyday life.

A garden is a dried wreath on the door or a potted geranium on the windowsill. It is the container garden climbing up the steps to your front door. It is the flower-draped lane you pass on your daily walks. It is where a twirling little girl plucks the petals of a flower, chanting "he loves me, he loves me not." It is the dramatic ten-year-old spider plant that drapes from your ceiling. It is the public garden where you spend your lunch break. It is at your back door. It is a touchstone of creation, a reminder of our inheritance, and a gift for those to come.

The world is a garden created for you to bask in and be loved. It is a place of cooperation and wonder. It is where you find the love note written to you from the Creator of the universe who formed you in His likeness and viewed your splendor as the pinnacle of creation.

Acknowledgments

Carrie Gress and Noelle Mering are perhaps the most extraordinary mentors a woman could hope to have. This book would not be if it were not for their vision and loving guidance. To Brian Kennelly and the entire team at TAN Books whose work changes the world one book at a time. To my parents, who filled my childhood with beauty and gave me my first "bit of earth."

Bibliography

Backhouse, Janet. *The Isabella Breviary*. British Library Board, 1993.

Don, Monty. *The Complete Gardener*. Second Edition. Penguin Random House, 2021.

Ferri, Laurent and Helene Jacquemard. *The Tres Riches Heures du duc de Berry*. Paris: Skira, 2018.

Rowen, Herbert H., Michael J. Wintle, Henk Meijer, and Marcus Willem Heslinga. "Dutch Civilization in the Golden Age (1609–1713)" Brittanica. https://www.britannica.com/place/Netherlands/Dutch-civilization-in-the-Golden-Age-1609-1713.

"The Book of Hours: A Medieval Bestseller." Metropolitan Museum of Art, June 2017.

"The History of Roses." University of Illinois. https://web.extension.illinois.edu/roses/history.cfm.

Thurston, Herbert. "St. Valentine." *The Catholic Encyclopedia*. Vol. 15. New York: Robert Appleton Company, 1912. Accessed 27 Oct. 2022.

Lockwood, Louise. Presented by Roger Scruton. "Why Beauty Matters." 2009.

EMILY MALLOY'S floral design career began as an apprentice who swept petals and leaves off the floors of a rapidly growing floral shop in Philadelphia. She eventually rose to manager and floral designer. Her work has appeared in *Elle Décor* and *Green Wedding Shoes*, and she is currently the food and floral design editor at TheologyofHome.com. She and her husband live in Mississippi with their four children.